The Humanities in
the Age of Information
and Post-Truth

The Humanities in the Age of Information and Post-Truth

✦

Edited by Ignacio López-Calvo
and Christina Lux

NORTHWESTERN UNIVERSITY PRESS

EVANSTON, ILLINOIS

Northwestern University Press
www.nupress.northwestern.edu

Printed in the United States of America

10 9 8 7 6 5 4 3 2 1

Library of Congress Cataloging-in-Publication Data

Names: López-Calvo, Ignacio, editor. | Lux, Christina (Christina Anne), editor.
Title: The humanities in the age of information and post-truth / edited by Ignacio
   López-Calvo and Christina Lux.
Description: Evanston, Illinois : Northwestern University Press, 2019. | Includes
   index.
Identifiers: LCCN 2018035295 | ISBN 9780810139138 (cloth : alk. paper) | ISBN
   9780810139121 (pbk. : alk. paper) | ISBN 9780810139145 (ebook)
Subjects: LCSH: Humanities—Study and teaching (Higher)—United States.
Classification: LCC AZ183.U5 H845 2019 | DDC 001.3071/173—dc23
LC record available at https://lccn.loc.gov/2018035295

To my mother, María Teresa Calvo Matesanz (I.L.-C.)

CONTENTS

The Humanities in
the Age of Information
and Post-Truth

Introduction

The Humanities Today

Ignacio López-Calvo

By post-humanities I mean . . . the posing of alternative
modalities for taking up, for doing, for engaging (and for an
engaging) humanities. Post-humanities speak to the ways in
which the material and conceptual conditions establishing the
conventions by which humanities once were structured and
recognized no longer obtain. These conventional assumptions,
ways of doing the humanities, and of being a (professional)
humanist are at best now an elusive nostalgia. The "post-
humanities" are a siren call, accordingly, for another way
of engaging humanities, that speak to the living and deathly
conditions of our moment.

—David Theo Goldberg, "The Afterlife of the Humanities"

The Book and Its Structure

The essays in this volume address the place of the humanities amid the
ontological and epistemological uncertainties constantly produced in a
fast-changing world.[1] They explain their importance and value in the university and the world within the context of today's changing sociopolitical
landscape. While the reader may suspect that these types of lucubration
are a desperate reaction to the decreased public funding for the humanities worldwide, diminishing enrollments, or anxiety over the future of our

profession, a coherent argument is made in these essays for the continued need, now more than ever, to invest in humanities education, if we are to have well-informed citizens rather than just willing consumers and obedient workers.

This volume represents, therefore, a defense of the social and civic function of the humanities in today's democratic society while revealing their worth beyond their intrinsic and nonfunctional value. They are a valuable tool to address many of the large challenges that have arisen in the twenty-first century.

K. Anthony Appiah's opening essay, "For the Humanities," explores the distinctive character of learning in the humanities. He argues, as Hazlitt does in regard to the arts, that the humanities "are not progressive," meaning that art from the remote past remains important to us, in ways that ancient science does not, and work in the humanities presupposes that it continues to be worth studying cultural objects from long ago. More recently, adds Appiah, it has become clear that the humanities are inevitably transnational, in part because many of its objects of study emerge from transcultural interactions. By considering a passage from Cicero's defense of the poet Archias, he argues that we must see humanistic learning as an inevitable part of the preparation for a life as free citizens, because it trains us for the ethical reflection that is necessary if we are to lead meaningful lives. Appiah also underscores the centrality of the idiographic to the humanities, that is, the importance of understanding particular objects and not just universal truths, which he exemplifies by exploring the particularity of certain ideas contained in Montaigne's *Essays*.

In "Uberizing the University," David Theo Goldberg explores how American universities have changed since the late 1980s as a result of conservative legislatures that shrank budgets for public higher education and repealed affirmative action. Deepening the problem, the human interface of learning continues to be downsized through online teaching, which has contributed to less intellectual and demographic diversity on our campuses. He warns us about the end result of a faceless future with teacherless courses.

David Palumbo-Liu's "Rationality, Racism, and Imagining Social Justice" addresses these issues as reflected in recent national and international events. For instance, the recent decision of grand juries not to indict Darren Wilson for the killing of Michael Brown Jr. and the New York City police officer who put a chokehold on Eric Garner for several seconds until he died have produced in many a similar sense of disbelief and outrage. The same reaction was elicited by the Israeli attack on Gaza and the murders of the Charlie Hebdo staff, the slaughter of thousands in Nigeria, and the ISIL attacks in Paris in November 2015. Although the ideal of a racism-free world is certainly not going to happen any time soon, Palumbo-Liu argues that we need to think about how our study of the humanities can help us to move closer to being less hateful and unjust. His essay focuses on this idea of reasonableness and rationality as delivered in language, arguing that sometimes language leads us astray, obscures a clear vision of truth and justice, and fails to capture the human significance of injustice and to succeed in forming lines of solidarity. It is in struggling to find forms of adequacy, Palumbo-Liu argues, that the humanities can help us imagine social justice and imagine a politically effective negative dialectic.

Robert D. Newman's "Rage and Beauty: Celebrating Complexity, Democracy, and the Humanities" argues that the core methodologies of the humanities—interrogating and bridging—are mutually connected and are fundamental to a thriving, democratic culture. For the humanities to protect its future from adversarial neoliberal rhetoric and practices, a more substantive turn in its public engagement mission and practice is essential. Since the grand challenges and questions of our time require multiple perspectives and deeply contextualized solutions, we must insist on bringing a humanistic lens to a search for solutions, calling the public's attention to the humanities moments that reside in the profound junctures of personal and community experience. These moments help us to celebrate the complexity found at the heart of democracy and to rejoice in the bridging as well, the knitting together of contradictions that the humanities embody. Further, Newman problematizes the false dichotomy that exists between public humanities and "pure research."

David Castillo and William Egginton's "What Kind of Humanities Do We Want or Need in the Twenty-First Century?" proposes that nowadays the bigger question might not be what is it that we can do to rescue the arts and the humanities from their alleged crisis, but rather what can the arts and the humanities do to rescue society from the epidemic of anti-smarts denialism that has taken hold of public discourse? Castillo and Egginton argue that engaged and engaging humanities can help us break through the walls of the media bubble that treats intellectualism with impatience and suspicion while offering cover to the special interests invested in ignoring or denying such uncomfortable realities as global warming and structural injustice. Reading Cervantes's powerful diagnoses of his time and placing his works in the context of self-reflective humanities classes, they argue, can help us recognize our "glass cage"—in Nicholas Carr's evocative language—and possibly fight back against the dangers of anti-intellectual denialism.

Mariët Westermann's chapter, "The Humanities in the World: A Field Report," suggests ways in which the humanities can overcome the purported crisis. One successful way, according to Westermann, is to make our disciplines more worldly and civically engaged through public and community-engaged humanities. The examples she provides—dealing with refugee and immigrant studies as well as a retooling of local museums in consonance with new immigration waves—are a powerful reminder of all the work that remains to be done and of how critical humanities training can help solve some of humanities' more pressing challenges.

The volume closes with an afterword by Doris Sommer, "Keywords: A Refresher on Humanism and Praxis," which returns to the opening question of the ethical and civic relevance of the humanities in today's world. Sommer offers keywords as entry points to new theoretical material, novel ideas, and ways of thinking. We invite readers—students, researchers, and members of the general public—to build on her proposed lexicon and to take these keywords as launching points for imagining, discussing, and mapping a future for the arts and humanities, not only in the United States but also around the world.

The Humanities

Defining the humanities is not easy. Goldberg posits that the humanities translate "the human to ourselves: what it is to be, what it means and has meant to be, and what it ought to be human." Laying bare the human condition in the past, present and future, exploring—beyond the traditional disciplines of languages, literature, philosophy, and history—individual and collective identification in changing conditions as revealed in texts, practices, values, and other venues and media (the internet, computer games, television, radio, advertising) is essential to the humanities. Goldberg writes, "I want to mark the domain of the humanities more abstractly and capaciously as any analytic and critical engagement with questions of meaning, value, and significance, whatever their modes, media and histories of expression or sites of reference, materialization, or objectification."[2] This explains the prefix "post-" in this introduction's epigraph.

The humanities are often conflated with the liberal arts; they are grouped with the arts and the analytical or humanistic social sciences. Although, as Goldberg argues, the greater humanities must go beyond traditional academic disciplines, the humanities are traditionally associated with the analysis of languages (linguistics, philology), literature, history, jurisprudence, philosophy, comparative religion, ethics, visual and performing arts, and critical theory. The boundary between the humanities and the social sciences is at times blurred when dealing with history, archaeology, anthropology, area studies, communication studies, classical studies, law, and linguistics. Humanistic approaches to objects of study, such as human phenomena, cultures, expression, behavior, and past and present societies, help us to connect with other contemporary and historical humans. They record and try to understand the present and the history of human beings, helping us to make sense of our complex world and to envision our future life. They guide us through the history of ideas and consciousness.

Post-Truth and the Importance of the Humanities

What is the value and importance of the humanities in these times of Trumpism and the prevalence of post-truth? The so-called post-truth or post-factual politics refers to a new political culture wherein factual rebuttals are ignored or considered unimportant, instead focusing exclusively on emotional appeals and talking points. This tendency has been strengthened by the preponderance of social media and ratings-focused twenty-four-hour news networks. The concept is related to the American comedian Stephen Colbert's idea of "truthiness" in contemporary political discourse, that is, the tendency to characterize something as true only because one has a "gut feeling" about it. Intuition supersedes evidence and facts. Although he coined the term in 2005, the concept of "truthiness" regained its centrality during the 2016 U.S. presidential campaign. For example, on November 30, 2016, President-elect Donald Trump's surrogate Scottie Nell Hughes openly stated during an interview on National Public Radio's *Diane Rehm Show* that objective facts no longer exist:

There are no such things as facts. . . . Well, I think it's also an idea
of an opinion. And that's—on one hand I hear half the media saying that these are lies, but on the other half there are many people
that go, no, it's true. . . . And so one thing that has been interesting
this entire campaign season to watch is that people that say facts
are facts, they're not really facts. . . . There's no such thing, unfortunately, anymore as facts. And so Mr. Trump's tweets, amongst a
certain crowd—a large part of the population—are truth. When he
says that millions of people illegally voted, he has some—amongst
him and his supporters, and people believe they have facts to back
that up. Those that do not like Mr. Trump, they say that those are lies,
and there's no facts to back it up.[3]

Objective facts and subjective opinion seem to have suddenly blended into
one. Then, on December 4, 2016, when outgoing Republican National
Committee chairman and upcoming White House chief of staff Reince
Priebus was asked on CBS's *Face the Nation* about Trump's outlandish
comments regarding voter fraud and millions of illegal votes cast during
the presidential election, he argued, without evidence to support these
claims, that it was indeed possible and that the president-elect was just
"pushing the envelope."[4] Along these lines, when George Stephanopou-
los on ABC's *This Week* asked Vice President–elect Mike Pence about
Trump's comments, Pence answered, "He's entitled to express his opinion on that. And I think the American people find it very refreshing that
they have a president who will tell them what's on his mind."[5] To openly
defend falsehoods before the American public has therefore become a
"refreshing" development, according to Pence, because Trump "speaks
his mind." Speaker of the House Paul Ryan later worsened matters on
the December 4 edition of *60 Minutes* by telling journalist Scott Pelley
that fake news and the veracity of the president-elect's statements are
unimportant: "It doesn't matter to me. He won the election. . . . The way
I see the tweets you're talking about, he's basically giving voice to a lot of
people who have felt that they were voiceless. He's communicating with
people in this country who've felt like they have not been listened to. He's
going to be an unconventional president."[6]

Indeed on November 8, 2016, the world seemed to flip for many
Americans, for residents in the United States, and, by extension, for the
world at large. The candidate of the Republican Party, Donald J. Trump,

a climate-change denier who promised to build a wall at the border with Mexico, to make a registry of Muslims in the United States and to forbid U.S. entry to Muslims, to reverse *Roe v. Wade* and end the Affordable Care Act, among other controversial statements, and whose campaign managed to garner the support of strange bedfellows such as the Ku Klux Klan and Russian president Vladimir Putin's KGB, unexpectedly won the presidential election. Apparently the election of Barack Obama, the first African American U.S. president, did not mean that we now live in a post-racial America.

Many wondered how this could happen. What is there to do when most statistics, polls, and data failed in their projections? Eric Klinenberg, a professor of sociology and director of the Institute for Public Knowledge at New York University, has criticized our "excessive faith in Big-Data analytics, and insufficient concern about the quality of the data we're producing," worrying that "the Big Data revolution may go too far, pulling resources away from other valuable forms of knowledge production, such as ethnography, history, and philosophy."[7] As a reaction to these Big Data flaws, journalists have recently begun to interview working-class studies scholars in an attempt to figure out the origin of the anger that supposedly pushed white working-class voters to become Trump base voters. In campus conversations, some of my humanities colleagues wondered if cultural and sociological studies should focus more on this sector of the population that feels disenfranchised. It is clear that not everything can be quantified. Other types of research, including humanistic scholarship, can be far more insightful; keeping in mind a group's social memory and self-definition or empathizing with its historical disenfranchisement, for example, can shape our understanding of human behavior.

The shocking U.S. presidential election results have only added to the uncertainty and befuddlement produced by Brexit (the United Kingdom's withdrawal from the European Union), following an advisory referendum held in June 2016, which has adversely affected the U.K. economy and exposed deep social divisions in British society between educated urbanites and rural populations, as is occurring in the United States. Paradoxically this Brexit, supported by certain British conservatives, has inspired some frustrated, progressive Californians to fill social media with talk about a potential Calexit and to display a new flag for California with the phrase "New California Republic." Using the hashtag #CalExit, the small movement—claiming that California, the sixth largest economy in the world, is relatively self-sufficient—proposes to secede from the United States (or to join Canada) and is being partially funded by Shervin Pishevar, an early investor in Uber, and other tech supporters. This argument appears on their website: "As the sixth largest economy in the world, California is more economically powerful than France and has a population larger than Poland. Point by point, California compares and competes with countries, not just the 49 other states."[8] The Yes California Independence Campaign claims that in the spring of 2019, Californians will go to the polls to decide whether the state should exit the Union and achieve its independence.

In Austria, the very narrow victory (49.7 percent vs. 50.3 percent) of Alexander Van der Bellen, the son of two refugees and a former Green Party leader running as an independent, prevented the victory of his far-right opponent, the Freedom Party's Norbert Hofer, in the presidential election in May 2016. In the wake of the refugee crisis, Hofer, like Brexit proponents, ran on an anti-immigrant, Euroskeptic platform. Austria therefore became the second country to elect a Green candidate (after Latvia); had Hofer won, it would have been the first European country to elect a far-right head of state.

Beyond the West, the victory in the Philippines' May 9, 2016, presidential election of Rodrigo Duterte, who openly supports extrajudicial killings of drug dealers, users, petty criminals, and street children by vigilante groups, is perhaps less shocking than the fact that a poll conducted by Pulse Asia in July 2016 found that 91 percent of Filipinos actually trust Duterte, making him their most trusted politician since these surveys began. Back in the U.S. after the presidential election, during a television appearance on the show *Fox and Friends*, former House speaker and Trump supporter Newt Gingrich publicly called for the creation of a new House Committee on Un-American Activities, with the pretext of ridding the country of American ISIS adherents and sympathizers. Overall it has become clear that all sorts of populism are on the rise in the United States, Europe, Latin America, and the rest of the world. Is the climate of the 1930s back again? One has to wonder. Is the world turned upside down? We may be able to find valuable answers and solutions in humanistic research and teaching.

In a recent article titled "Education and Activist Humanities, Now More Than Ever," Palumbo-Liu argues for the civic value of activist humanities in the wake of the results of the 2016 presidential elections:

When we put forward any discussion of topics such as ethics, social justice, gender, sexuality, race, religion, culture, we need to place those discussions in the context of our new contemporary situation. In so doing we may often find ourselves taking a stance in opposition to the prevailing ideology. I recommend we embrace that oppositionality and form lines of solidarity with others. We need to see how rational and civil discourse and self-reflective contemplation are necessary tools when we increasingly hear that they are inconvenient and dispensable niceties. In so doing we make a renewed and intensified commitment to the very idea of humanity and the greater good. We must adapt our point of reference according to this new historical situation.[9]

Palumbo-Liu encourages educators to embrace their commitment to civil discourse and activism as a tool against ignorance and bigotry. Likewise, Michael Flood, along with others, proposes different ways in which academia can be a site for activism: "(1) as a means to produce knowledge to inform progressive social change; (2) as a means for conducting research which itself involves social change; (3) as a site for progressive strategies of teaching and learning; and finally (4) as an institution whose power relations themselves may be challenged and reconstructed."[10] Simultaneously he laments the lack of interest in activist scholarship among the most prestigious journals, as well as the fact that certain types of activism may threaten academic advancement.

Palumbo-Liu refuses the rhetoric of increased enrollment and majors as the correct measure of value for the humanities. Instead, he asserts, we should recognize what he calls the nonacademic "invisible humanities," that is, the "arts, music, literature, philosophy, et cetera that circulate in the public sphere unattended to and unrecognized by academic measurements,"[11] as a way to connect with a young public. By contrast, Bruce Cole, who served as chair of the National Endowment for the Humanities from 2001 until 2009, has argued precisely against activist humanities research: "Many of the applications were also heavily weighted toward the advocacy of one cause or another. The NEH charter forbids the funding of such applications, but it would be a mistake not to see them as a reflection of the weaponization of the academic humanities for the promotion of social or political agendas, something I'm sure we all frown upon."[12]

Likewise, in "There Is No Such Thing as Western Civilization," Appiah reminds us that not only is "Western culture" a fairly recent invention but that the values of liberty, tolerance, and rational inquiry are not uniquely Western:

> Values aren't a birthright: you need to keep caring about them. Living in the west, however you define it, being western, provides no guarantee that you will care about western civilisation. The values European humanists like to espouse belong just as easily to an African or an Asian who takes them up with enthusiasm as to a European. By that very logic, of course, they do not belong to a European who has not taken the trouble to understand and absorb them. The same, of course, is true in the other direction. The story of the golden nugget suggests that we cannot help caring about the traditions of "the west" because they are ours: in fact, the opposite is true. They are only ours if we care about them. A culture of liberty, tolerance, and rational inquiry: that would be a good idea. But these values represent choices to make, not tracks laid down by a western destiny.[13]

Indeed in this book we argue that humanistic education is a valuable tool to strengthen these intercultural values in our societies, which are not, as Appiah points out, inherently Western. Recent European history shows us that these values can be replaced by authoritarianism, racism, xenophobia, misogyny, homophobia, bigotry, and intolerance. Moreover the teleology of a human history as a permanently positive progress and evolution is a myth: when neglected, liberties and rights, including the freedom of the press, are lost throughout the world. Democracy is an exception rather than the rule in the history of human societies.

On the other hand, the humanities and the arts are not a luxury but an integral part of a complete scholarly education. It is undeniable that, without the humanities, we will never have fully educated students or real universities; instead we will be dealing with instrumentalist corporate research centers or technical training institutions, as explained in Newman's essay in this volume. And, of course, besides their inherent worth, the humanities continue to have a key social role in public life, in the pursuit of social justice, in the empowerment of marginalized communities, in the defense of human rights, and in the encouragement of tolerance and intercultural understanding. After all, as Patrícia Vieira points out, "Neither a dying set of disciplines nor a panacea for social ills, the humanities remain a central form of human enquiry, in that they shed light on and question the tacit assumptions upon which our societies are based, outline the history of these values, and identify alternatives to the status quo."[14] Along these lines, as Klinenberg suggests, humanities and social sciences professors could become instrumental in teaching our students how to navigate information in social media:

> Like it or not, social media is at the center of the new public sphere. This election leaves no doubt that candidates, campaigns, and their surrogates can make great use of it: planting memes, spreading rumors, building communities. Professors know how to help students work through difficult ideas in books and articles. But except for some of us in the learning sciences, few of us have thought much about how to help students develop critical-thinking skills for the media that they use most.[15]

Even the economic argument for the humanities holds, as the data prove, that they are major economic drivers of many institutions of higher education. Often in the name of global economic competitiveness, there is a renewed commitment to STEM (science, technology, engineering, and mathematics) education and an emphasis on professional training programs, such as for business, law, computer sciences, and engineering. Yet, as Peter Mandler, a professor of modern cultural history at the University of Cambridge, states, "It might not be good economic policy to steer students to STEM—education alone can't create demand for skills, and too many STEM graduates could mean only too many underemployed (and dissatisfied) STEM graduates."[16]

Again, students without sufficient language knowledge and foreign culture familiarity or without appropriate analytic, writing, and oral skills that a humanities education can provide will be ill-prepared for an increasingly globalized world with a competitive workforce. More important, as mentioned, the humanities continue to have social and civic relevance, as a globally oriented, well-rounded, well-informed, well-educated citizenry, capable of independent, critical thinking and analysis may improve the functioning of a true democratic society. Familiarity with different and alternative ways of being in the world throughout history, which a humanities education can provide, makes us more tolerant, compassionate, and ready to face planetary challenges. It may also help us to navigate times of crisis and to make sense of the world whenever it seems as if it were topsy-turvy. Awareness of human diversity, fluency in other languages and cultures, and an understanding of how they shape our worldviews all contribute to having more pluralistic campuses and more open-minded societies.

It is important to keep in mind that the humanities and the sciences should not be perceived as alternatives or as enemies; the truth is that they complement each other, as we need multiple perspectives to answer the big questions and problems of our times, including social injustice, racial inequality, and the biggest of them all: human survival in the face of climate change and its attempted cover-up by the neoliberal media and certain market-obsessed political institutions. It is often said that, while the sciences answer the "how" and "what," the humanities tend to be better equipped to answer the "why." Humanistic instruction can provide key independent, critical thinking tools to stop climate change before it is too late, rather than limiting ourselves to studying its effects. They can also change the discourse about air and water pollution as a human rights issue and problematize the capitalist imperative of conspicuous consumption and planned obsolescence before all life on our planet is negatively affected and the extinction of animal species becomes even more extreme than it is currently. But the humanities and the sciences also complement each other in practical economic ways. For instance, in a recent article, the *Wall Street Journal*'s small business expert David Kalt stated that his experience has proven that a liberal arts education produces better programmers: "My point isn't that we don't need qualified, formally trained engineers with university degrees. Rather, I'm suggesting that if more tech hires held a philosophy or English degree with some programming on the side, we might in the end create better leaders in technology and life."[17]

Identifying Problems in Humanities Education and Research

It is no secret that declining enrollments among humanities majors and graduate students, along with a decrease in academic jobs in the humanistic disciplines in recent years, have been alarming. Heidi Tworek and Ben Schmidt have argued that the reason for this decline is the shift in women's academic choices: "Women started deserting subjects like history and

English decades ago."[18] The anti-intellectualism of these neoliberal times, in which market fundamentalism rejects whatever is not defined by the market as useless, has driven governments and university leaders to cut funding for our disciplines and programs (while exponentially increasing the number of university administrators nationwide, perhaps one of the real reasons for budget constraints), more so than for the other disciplines. Public opposition to public funding for education at all levels and to social programs in general, together with the neoliberal tendency to privatize and to be suspicious of any type of government funding for public programs or institutions other than for the military, the police, and sports venues, has not helped the humanities. On the other hand, today's American universities' dependency on fundraising means that, if we are not vigilant, our programs and research may end up increasingly reshaped in unforeseeable ways.

The typical narrative for these measures, as mentioned, tends to claim that the humanities are not practical, as they do not prepare our students for the marketplace or for the real world. The same market logic also argues that the humanities are often subsidized by other disciplines when, in fact, the opposite may be true. Indeed, although administrators rarely emphasize it, as they tend to focus on our disciplines' failure to attract external funding and endowments, we often teach more students, as many of our disciplines are required, and, as is well known, tuition-fee revenue is a major income source. Fortunately in recent years humanities professors have become more proactive in problematizing these myths through public advocacy, in resituating themselves and the humanities as crucial to the educational mission of the university, and in proving the critical impact of the humanities on people's lives, including those of our students. But further advocacy needs to be included. Cole argues that humanities scholars need to provide a stronger argument in defense of their profession, starting at their own institutions: "The situation will not improve until those alarmed at what has happened to their field start making a case, beyond their own professional interests, for this essential part of our culture and society."[19] This book is an attempt to do so.

Potential Solutions to "The Crisis in the Humanities"

Mandler has denied the existence of an actual crisis in the humanities in the English-speaking world:

> It is worth making clear . . . that today, in a greatly expanded popula-
> tion, a reasonably stable share of all degrees translates to a greatly
> increased absolute number of students in the humanities. There are,
> simply, significantly more people with humanities educations than
> ever before. So it is hard to take too seriously talk of a crisis in the
> UK when, even by the narrowest definition of the humanities, the
> absolute number of such students has increased five-fold since 1967,
> and by a broader definition including new humanities fields almost
> ten-fold. In the US, over a period of much slower expansion, their
> numbers have still doubled.[20]

Likewise, in *Manifesto for the Humanities: Transforming Doctoral Education in Good Enough Times*, Sidonie A. Smith offers an optimistic
outlook guided by reform in graduate education through learning across
institutions and research programs. These large-scale humanities collaborations in multilocational universities connected by cyberinfrastructure,
she explains, increase the number of potential mentors and the synergies
among like-minded students. Smith has also called for "thinking outside
the box" by going beyond the dissertation monograph and expanding the
possible forms the doctoral dissertation might take, embracing more flex-
ible options such as a collection of essays, a digital project, a collection of
different genres of scholarly writing, public scholarship, a documentary, a
translation or textual edition, or a project-in-comics mode. Likewise, she
suggests alternatives to the seminar paper, including collaborative essays,
a grant application, a creative portfolio, a lecture for an undergraduate
survey course, glossaries, a mapping project, curation, or a blog edited
into a publishable piece.

  In any case, instead of obsessing with the decline of funding for the
humanities,[21] the constantly shrinking list of tenure-track jobs in our
disciplines,[22] or the diminishing number of humanities students,[23] it is
more productive to insist on the benefits (all kinds, not only economic)
of a humanities education for individuals as well as society in general.
An increased emphasis on open access and public humanities, including
digital humanities, has contributed to translating our research for the
increasingly skeptical general public, educating citizens about the true
significance of humanistic research and teaching. Taking advantage of
the "digital turn," which has the potential of reinvigorating humanistic
scholarship, we can combat stereotypes that categorize the humanities

as an obscure, arcane, solipsistic, and esoteric endeavor, which tends to be overly politicized. Against the neoliberal market-impact arguments, which turn university chancellors and presidents into CEOs, students into consumers, and campuses into marketplaces, we can argue that the humanities offer more adaptable skills for different professions (improvements in writing and oral communication as well as in the ability to develop thorough argumentation, for example).

Humanistic research is also justified by the creation of new knowledge in all disciplines (humanistic or not), which in itself supports its inherent value. And of course students may well choose to pursue a liberal arts education in search of self-fulfillment, knowledge, intellectual development, or an improved quality of life, regardless of its potential financial return; after all, the university is supposed to serve other purposes (hopefully higher purposes) beyond job training and economic growth. As cliché as it may sound, we must undoubtedly learn from past historical events to avoid making similar mistakes in the future: the socioeconomic and cultural conditions that led to the rise of fascism and colonialism may resurface, and past events may help us prevent likely outcomes. As Goldberg evocatively put it:

> It is all this that the humanities especially—what I want to characterize as the post-humanities, the afterlife of the humanities that once were and no longer are sustainable—could and should have a special standing, an opportunity and obligation, to address and to which to contribute. To identify the lived conditions of our time, to make them clear. To genealogize and historicize their coming to be and their cultural articulations. To understand how the structural patterns and variations have come to be, how they constitute part of, as they are constituted by, a broader social map. To suggest different ways of getting at our lived and death-producing conditions, to ask new questions about them. To reveal dynamic and productive ways of understanding and responding to these conditions.[24]

The media theorist and philosopher Geert Lovink has also argued for going beyond conventional or traditional humanities studies to update the disciplines by incorporating technology, studies on technology (social media, multimedia), and technology-mediated political participation (the use of Twitter during the Arab Spring and the Occupy Movement, for

example): "Instead of fighting for 'liberal arts' as antidote [to the sci-
ences] I would argue to bring out, to play out, the technological in the
humanities, and stop seeing them as opposites. Painting is a technique, so
is dancing. Writing is. These are basic insights of media theory that are
apparently not shared by everyone." Lovink suggests a new approach to
study and to understand sociocultural trends: "Our culture is a digital
culture. We cannot leave that out of the equation, and only blame the
low profit-driven motives. We can no longer call for the imagination. The
imagination has gone technical. Thoughtful individuals express themselves in ones and zeros."[25] It has become apparent that a humanities'
or post-humanities' challenge is to include new media, become digitally
literate, and mobilize the tools to translate historical as well as contemporary conditions. These new digital tools will help us to understand the
human condition and how we express it, what makes us human and what
the overall meaning of being human is. The humanities and the arts can
play a key role in mediating local, national, and international issues of
our day, in analyzing complicated human experiences, along with providing a human face or considering the human dimensions of research in
other academic fields (not that other disciplines are inhuman or that the
humanities are the only means to achieve those goals). Thus Christina H.
Paxson, the president of Brown University, posits:

> As many previous generations have learned, innovations in science
> and technology are tremendously important. But they inevitably result
> in unintended consequences. Some new inventions, if only available to
> small numbers, increase inequity or competition for scarce resources,
> with multiplying effects. We need humanists to help us understand
> and respond to the social and ethical dimensions of technological
> change. As more changes come, we will need humanists to help us
> filter them, calibrate them, and when necessary, correct them.[26]

Open-access publications, interdisciplinary research (including across the
sciences and engineering fields) and the digital humanities, which enhance
humanities research through digital technology, can help us disseminate
our research and reach a global audience. The more we expose humanistic research to a wider public, by any possible means, including op-eds
and social media, the more opportunity we have to attract public funding and appreciation for our work. Likewise more recent approaches to

humanistic inquiry, taking advantage of affect theory and the applications of neuroscience research or of data-mining methods, have opened up exciting new paths for our scholarship.

Another promising development is the renewed emphasis on community-engaged humanities or public humanities, which propose ethical, sustainable, engaged research *with* (rather than *for* or *on*) the community. Community-engaged humanities are supposed to respond to a commitment to the public good, including for the benefit of groups traditionally exploited and recolonized by university researchers, such as indigenous people. This last type of research has the potential of being more helpful to indigenous communities when university scholars share their research findings with them. Civic engagement involves genuine, nonhierarchical exchanges of expertise between university actors and community partners in order to carry out research and teaching on key social, public issues. Mutual respect and the production of new knowledge that is relevant to both the campus and the public are fundamental for the success of these partnerships. However, more institutional support for public scholarship, together with a rewards system in tenure and promotion considerations, are needed, as community-engaged scholars are often punished for such time-consuming activities. From this perspective, Diane C. Calleson, Nancy Cantor, Steven Lavine, and others have suggested the implementation of a different assessment approach, by which the peer-reviewed article and the single-author monograph are no longer the only outcomes accepted.[27] Cantor and Lavine allow instead for more collaborative and interdisciplinary paradigms: "We are recommending that faculty members and evaluators not advise junior colleagues to postpone public scholarship if that is where their passions lie. We must take public scholarship seriously and frame broader and more-flexible definitions of scholarship, research, and creative work."[28]

As early as 1996 Ernest L. Boyer lamented, "Almost every college catalog in this country still lists teaching, research, and service as the priorities of the professoriate; yet, at tenure and promotion time, the harsh truth is that service is hardly mentioned. And even more disturbing, faculty who do spend time with so-called applied projects frequently jeopardize their careers."[29] He encourages academics to participate more actively, as intellectuals, in public discourse and in civic advancement. Without this scholarship of engagement, campuses will continue to be viewed by the general public only as a place where students obtain their degrees and professors build their careers, thus remaining irrelevant to the nation's problems (and the world's problems, I would add). Boyer therefore recommends broadening the scope of scholarship by incorporating the "application of knowledge,"[30] making knowledge useful, aiming toward more humane ends, and moving from theory to practice, and then back to theory.

From a different perspective, Rosi Braidotti, in *The Posthuman*'s fourth chapter, "Posthuman Humanities: Life beyond Theory," proposes to move away from a self-centered anthropocentric framework, focusing instead on species egalitarianism. She argues for decentering "Man" as the measure of all things and for embracing more planetary intellectual challenges. In her own words, "Over the last thirty years, new critical epistemologies have offered alternative definitions of the 'human' by inventing interdisciplinary areas which call themselves 'studies,' like: gender, feminism, ethnicity, cultural studies, post-colonial, media and new media and Human rights studies." Braidotti proposes new epistemological foundations for the reinvigoration of the humanities, arguing, "Technologically mediated post-anthropocentrism can enlist the resources of bio-genetic codes, as well as telecommunication, new media and information technologies, to the task of renewing the Humanities. Posthuman subjectivity reshapes the identity of humanistic practices, by stressing heteronomy and multi-faceted relationality, instead of autonomy and self-referential disciplinary purity."[31] She points to interdisciplinary areas of success across the post-anthropocentric humanities, such as animal studies, ecocriticism, and disability studies, which are symptomatic of the vitality of the field.

Conclusion

Among the many personal, social, and global benefits that can be provided by a liberal arts education, the humanities are suited for global citizenship, for cultivating well-informed citizens, and for the appreciation of aesthetic values that may lead us to a more meaningful life and a curiosity for cultural understanding. As John Horgan explains, the humanities deal more with questions than answers; they teach us healthy skepticism and uncertainty; they teach us to question authority: "The humanities are subversive. They undermine the claims of all authorities, whether political, religious or scientific. This skepticism is especially important when it comes to claims about humanity, about what we are, where we came from, and even what we can be and *should* be." Horgan adds that the humanities "keep us from being trapped by our own desire for certainty."[32] The essays that follow eloquently argue for these and other benefits that humanistic inquiry can add to our lives and our democratic societies.

Notes

1. This project emerges out of more than two years of sponsored research at the University of California, Merced, on the topic "The World Upside Down," including a biweekly seminar, a conference, and the Distinguished Lecture in the Humanities series.
2. Goldberg, "The Afterlife of the Humanities."
3. Ursulafaw, "'There Are No Such Things as Facts.'"
4. Benen, "Trump Allies."
5. Ibid.
6. Lithwick and Tsai, "Actually, Paul Ryan."
7. Klinenberg, "What Trump's Win."
8. Robinson, "Californians Are Calling for a 'Calexit.'"
9. Palumbo-Liu, "Education and Activist Humanities."
10. Flood et al., "Combining Academia and Activism," 17.
11. Palumbo-Liu, "Education and Activist Humanities."
12. Cole, "What's Wrong with the Humanities?"
13. Appiah, "There Is No Such Thing."
14. Vieira, "What Are the Humanities For?"
15. Klinenberg, "What Trump's Win."
16. Mandler, "Rise of the Humanities."
17. Kalt, "Why I Was Wrong."
18. Tworek, "The Real Reason."
19. Cole, "What's Wrong with the Humanities?"
20. Mandler, "Rise of the Humanities."
21. "In comparison to other fields, academic humanities research and development in 2012 was more likely to be funded either by educational institutions themselves or by not-for-profit entities. Academic institutions supplied 59% of the funding for humanities research, while the federal government provided 20%. In the education, engineering, and science fields, more than 55% of academic research funding came from the federal government." American Academy of Arts and Sciences, "The State of the Humanities," 18.
22. "In 2012, less than half of the humanities faculty members were employed off the tenure track. The percentage of faculty employed off the tenure track ranged from 19% in history of science programs (which tended to be situated in specialized doctoral-level programs at research universities) to almost 50% in the communication and language disciplines." Ibid., 15.

23. "After almost two decades in which the share of all new bachelor's degrees conferred on students in the humanities had been stable, the percentage dropped from 12% in 2007 to approximately 10% in 2013. The shares of degrees awarded to humanities students at other levels each followed different trajectories from 1987 to 2013. The share of degrees conferred at the master's degree level has been in an extended period of gradual decline (from a high of 4.6% in 1993 to 3.2% in 2013). Over the same span, the share at the doctoral level peaked at 10.5% in 2000, fell as low as 7.3% in 2007, and then rose to 8.4% in 2012 before slipping to 8.2% in 2013." Ibid., 6.

24. Goldberg, "The Afterlife of the Humanities."

25. Lovink, "On Martha Nussbaum's *Not for Profit*."

26. Paxson, "The Economic Case."

27. Calleson et al., "Community-Engaged Scholarship"; Cantor and Lavine, "Taking Public Scholarship Seriously."

28. Cantor and Lavine, "Taking Public Scholarship Seriously."

29. Boyer, "The Scholarship of Engagement," 18.

30. Ibid., 23.

31. Braidotti, *The Posthuman*, 144, 145.

32. Horgan, "Why Study Humanities?"

Works Cited

American Academy of Arts and Sciences. "The State of the Humanities: Higher Education 2015." *Humanities Indicators*. Accessed March 28, 2016. http://www.humanitiesindicators.org/binaries/pdf/HI_HigherEd2015.pdf.

Appiah, Kwame Anthony. "There Is No Such Thing as Western Civilization." *The Guardian*, November 11, 2016. https://www.theguardian.com/world/2016/nov/09/western-civilisation-appiah-reith-lecture.

Benen, Steve. "Trump Allies Defend His Election Lie as 'Refreshing.'" MSNBC.com, December 5, 2016. http://www.msnbc.com/rachel-maddow-show/trump-allies-defend-his-election-lie-refreshing.

Boyer, Ernest L. "The Scholarship of Engagement." *Bulletin of the American Academy of Arts and Sciences* 49, no. 7 (1996): 18–33.

Braidotti, Rosi. *The Posthuman*. Cambridge, U.K.: Polity Press, 2013.

Calleson, Diane C., et al. "Community-Engaged Scholarship: Is Faculty Work in Communities a True Academic Enterprise?" *Academic Medicine* 40, no. 4 (2005): 317–21.

Cantor, Nancy, and Steven Lavine. "Taking Public Scholarship Seriously." *Chronicle of Higher Education*, June 9, 2006. http://www.chronicle.com/article/Taking-Public-Scholarship/22684.

Cole, Bruce. "What's Wrong with the Humanities?" *Witherspoon Institute: Public Discourse*, February 1, 2016. http://www.thepublicdiscourse.com/2016/02/16248/.

Flood, Michael, Bryan Martin, and Tania Dreher. "Combining Academia and Activism: Common Obstacles and Useful Tools." *Australian Universities' Review* 55, no. 1 (2013): 17–26.

Goldberg, David Theo. "The Afterlife of the Humanities." University of California Humanities Research Institute. April 2014. https://humafterlife.uchri.org.

Horgan, John. "Why Study Humanities? What I Tell Engineering Freshmen." *Scientific American,* June 2013. https://blogs.scientificamerican.com/cross-check/why-study-humanities-what-i-tell-engineering-freshmen/.

Kalt, David. "Why I Was Wrong about Liberal-Arts Majors." *Wall Street Journal,* June 1, 2016. https://blogs.wsj.com/experts/2016/06/01/why-i-was-wrong-about-liberal-arts-majors/.

Klinenberg, Eric. "What Trump's Win Compels Scholars to Do." *Chronicle of Higher Education: The Chronicle Review,* November 11, 2016. http://www.chronicle.com/article/What-Trump-s-Win-Compels/238389?cid=cp66.

Lithwick, Dahlia, and Robert L. Tsai. "Actually, Paul Ryan, the President's Words Do Matter." *Slate,* December 6, 2016. http://www.slate.com/articles/news_and_politics/jurisprudence/2016/12/paul_ryan_says_it_doesn_t_matter_when_trump_lies_on_twitter_that_s_garbage.html.

Lovink, Geert. "On Martha Nussbaum's *Not for Profit.*" *Institute of Network Cultures,* June 15, 2010. http://networkcultures.org/geert/2010/06/15/on-martha-nussbaums-not-for-profit/.

Mandler, Peter. "Rise of the Humanities." *Aeon,* December 17, 2015. https://aeon.co/essays/the-humanities-are-booming-only-the-professors-can-t-see-it.

Palumbo-Liu, David. "Education and Activist Humanities, Now More Than Ever." *Huffington Post,* November 10, 2016. https://www.huffingtonpost.com/david-palumboliu/education-and-activist-humanities-now-more-than-ever_b_12904122.html.

Paxson, Christina H. "The Economic Case for Saving the Humanities." *New Republic,* August 20, 2013. https://newrepublic.com/article/114392/christina-paxson-president-brown-humanities-can-save-us.

Robinson, Melia. "Californians Are Calling for a 'Calexit' from the US—Here's How a Secession Could Work." *Business Insider*, November 9, 2016. http://www.businessinsider.com/calexit-explainer-california-plans-to-secede-2016-11.

Smith, Sidonie A. *Manifesto for the Humanities: Transforming Doctoral Education in Good Enough Times.* Ann Arbor: University of Michigan Press, 2015.

Tworek, Heidi. "The Real Reason the Humanities Are 'in Crisis.'" *The Atlantic,* December 18, 2013. https://www.theatlantic.com/education/archive/2013/12/the-real-reason-the-humanities-are-in-crisis/282441/.

Ursulafaw. "'There Are No Such Things as Facts' Says Trump Surrogate on NPR." *Dailykos.com,* December 1, 2016. https://www.dailykos.com/stories/2016/12/1/1606134/--There-Are-No-Such-Things-As-Facts-Says-Trump-Surrogate-On-NPR.

Vieira, Patrícia. "What Are the Humanities For?" *Los Angeles Review of Books,* September 17, 2014. https://lareviewofbooks.org/article/humanities/#!.

For the Humanities

K. Anthony Appiah

"In looking back on the great works of genius in former times, we are sometimes disposed to wonder at the little progress which has since been made in poetry, and in the arts of imitation in general."[1] That's William Hazlitt—the great English essayist—at the beginning of the third of his *Lectures on English Poetry*, delivered at the Surrey Institution on London's Ludgate Hill early in 1818.[2] The subject of his lecture was the poetry of Shakespeare and Milton, and the puzzle Hazlitt was discussing is surely a real one: Why was the poetry of his day (as of ours) not *obviously* superior to the works of these two great English poets, in the way that so many other things in his day—from politics to medicine to the physical sciences—so clearly *were* superior to their Elizabethan and Restoration counterparts? In the page or two that follow, Hazlitt takes up the theme (and often borrows whole passages) from an essay first published in the *Morning Chronicle* on January 11 and 15, 1814, and republished in 1817 in his essay collection, *The Round Table*.[3] That well-known exploration was entitled "Why the Arts Are Not Progressive?—A Fragment."

The heart of Hazlitt's answer to this question is to be found pretty much word for word in each of these three places, so we know he must have liked it; and it's encapsulated in the three characteristic sentences that follow:

> What is mechanical, reducible to rule or capable of demonstration, is progressive, and admits of gradual improvement: what is not mechanical, or definite, but depends on feeling, taste, and genius, very soon becomes stationary or retrograde, and loses more than it gains by transfusion. The contrary opinion is a vulgar error which has grown up, like many others, from transferring an analogy of one kind to something quite distinct, without taking into the account the difference in the nature of the things, or attending to the difference

of the results. For most persons, finding what wonderful advances
have been made in biblical criticism, in chemistry, in mechanics, in
geometry, astronomy, &c., i.e. in things depending on mere inquiry
and experiment or on absolute demonstration, have been led hastily
to conclude that there was a general tendency in the efforts of the
human intellect to improve by repetition, and, in all other arts and
institutions, to grow perfect and mature by time.[4]

Hazlitt's prose—like his opinions—are not to everyone's taste. The Irish
barrister and litterateur Eaton Stannard Barrett, reviewing the lectures in
the *Quarterly Review* that summer, declared, "We are not aware that it
contains a single just observation, which has not been expressed by other
writers more briefly, more perspicuously, and more elegantly. . . . His
remarks on particular quotations are often injudicious; his general rea-
sonings, for the most part, unintelligible."[5] But Barrett was surely wrong
about this element of the *Lectures:* the idea is relatively original and it is
relatively easy to understand. We can expect progress, Hazlitt thinks, only
in domains "reducible to rule."

I'll return to Hazlitt's answer later and to some thoughts of my own
about his question. But let me point out first that in an age of magnificent
progress in the sciences, pure and applied, we humanists have to be able
to answer a different question, though one very like Hazlitt's and, I think,
connected to it. The knowledge we acquire, the learning we transmit, the
traditions we inherit and study and value, presuppose the continuing per-
tinence to us here and now of human artifacts made by others, long (and
not so long) ago and far (and not so far) away. Why?

Shakespeare would be an unreliable guide to contemporary politics.
Aristotle is only an obstacle to our understanding of biology. Even New-
ton's *Principia*—perhaps the greatest work of physics ever written—can
be safely ignored by the modern student of physics. Why do humanists
return to the past if what we seek is the truth? If Hazlitt's answer is right,
then one reason some of these objects remain worthy of our attention is
that they have a kind of excellence that has not been superseded. And that
would help with *our* question, since no reasonable person could deny that
we have good reason to pay attention to what is excellent.

But accepting Hazlitt's claim that the arts are not progressive would
not be enough to defend the continuing relevance of humanistic study
of the past. For by the humanities, clearly, we mean more than Hazlitt

meant by "poetry and the arts of imitation"; we mean, as I have recently suggested, not so much the production as the study of the arts, and also the study of the widest range of the cultural artifacts of human civilizations, past and present, including artifacts that no one would claim to find interesting because of their excellence. We humanists are interested not only in what is excellent in the culture of our own time but also in what is excellent in the culture of the long ago and far away; and also, sometimes, in what is not excellent at all.

In this essay, I shall mostly take up a defense of the study of the long ago, but in the age of globalization I think the message that we need a cosmopolitan education has been widely accepted, both here in the United States and around the world. So there is, perhaps, a ready audience for reflection on the arts of other places. Still, before turning to the study of the past, let me remind you of what you surely already know: in our increasingly culturally interconnected world, we won't be able to manage our relations with one another, whether in politics or economics or cultural life, unless we develop the habit of conversation across cultures. That conversation is not only necessary, it is, when conducted right, hugely rewarding. And because all culture is contaminated by connections across political boundaries, there is no way of understanding ourselves without understanding others as well.

I can make the point swiftly with a few examples. Johann Wolfgang von Goethe (1749–1832) is widely agreed to be Germany's greatest poet. One of his wonderful poetic cycles is named the *West-östlicher Divan*: it is inspired by the poetry of Hafez (1325/6–1389/90). Hafez's tomb in Shiraz is still a place of Persian pilgrimage. William Shakespeare (1564–1616) is now widely agreed to be England's greatest dramatist. Two of his important influences are Livy, a Roman born in Padua, from whom he got Menenius's parable of the belly in *Coriolanus,* and Petrarch, whose sonnets are part of the background for all the major English sonnets of his time. Finally—and from the other side of the world—consider Matsuo Bashō, the magnificent haiku master of the seventeenth century, who was shaped to a large degree by Zen Buddhism. Which means Siddhartha Gautama, the Buddha, is part of Bashō's heritage. The point, then, is that wherever you start in studying the cultural artifacts that humanists care about, you will soon be led across national boundaries. Parochialism in the humanities gets in the way of understanding.

But now let me turn to what we learn from the humanities' insistence
on the continuing relevance of the past; in doing so, it will turn out that
I am discussing some of the reasons for studying Bashō, Goethe, Hafez,
Livy, Petrarch, or Shakespeare.

The word "humanities" elicits from the random recesses of my memory
a passage from the beginning of an oration—delivered in 62 B.C.E.—in
defense of Archias, the poet, a passage I learned by heart in high school
when I was studying Latin literature. It's the record of a legal argument
delivered by the Roman philosopher, lawyer, and politician Marcus Tul-
lius Cicero. The issue in the case was whether Archias, who had been born
in Antioch and was a friend of Cicero's, was in fact a Roman citizen.[6] The
passage in question—it is one of those endless Ciceronian sentences—can
be roughly translated like this:

> For when Archias first left boyhood, and turned from those arts by
> which young boys are gradually molded *ad humanitatem*, he devoted
> himself to the study of writing, first of all at Antioch—for he was
> born there in a noble place—which was formerly a famous and rich
> city, abundant in the most learned men and the most liberal studies,
> and there he succeeded speedily in showing himself superior to all in
> talent and in fame.[7]

I've left the phrase "ad humanitatem" untranslated for the moment,
because I want to point to another passage, just a little earlier, where the
same phrase occurs: "In truth, all the arts which are relevant ad humanitatem, have something in common which links them, and are, as it were,
connected by a certain kinship to one another."[8]

Now Cicero uses the word "humanitas" and its cognates a great deal.
(Lewis and Short, the famous Latin dictionary, remarks in parentheses of
the first sense they give for the word *humanitas*, "for the most part only
in Cic.") And in *Pro Archia*, when he's asking the court to permit him
more freedom than usual in the manner of his speech, he flatters the jury
by speaking of "this concourse of most highly educated men, with this
humanitas of yours."[9] In a later passage where he addresses the judges
again, he says, "Let this name of poet, therefore, judges, be holy among
you, the most humane—humanissimos—of men, a name that none, not
even barbarians, have defiled."[10]

It's true, of course, that *humanitas* can mean just "human nature, humanity."[11] But it's clear enough that what Cicero has in mind here when he says "ad humanitatem" is a second sense of the term: "mental cultivation befitting a man, liberal education, good breeding, elegance of manners or language, refinement," as Lewis and Short have it. And, picking up on the mention of a liberal education there, let's remember the other phrase that goes with humanities: the liberal arts. Cicero, recall, refers to these when he says of Archias's native city of Antioch that it was "liberalissimisque studiis adfluenti," rich in the most liberal studies. The studia liberales were studies or enthusiasms or endeavors (to borrow from Lewis and Short again) "befitting a freeman."[12] When Cicero speaks of Archias's boyhood education as having molded him "ad humanitatem," then, he must mean that it had provided him with an upbringing befitting a gentleman, a free man; and he was assuming that such an education would produce a kind of cultivation and refinement eminently worth having.

We are naturally suspicious these days of these ways of marking distinction, because they refer to the contrast between the free man and the slave, between gentlemen and what Hazlitt's contemporaries would have called "the lower orders," the common crowd whose vulgar error Hazlitt was repudiating in the passage with which I began. So if, as the French sociologist Pierre Bourdieu once argued, the critical function of humane or literary cultivation were merely to distinguish us from the common people, the humanities would be an exercise in snobbism.

But Bourdieu's thesis is not, of course, the whole truth. That a humane education can permit you to show off, I don't want to deny. So can long practice in golf, but that's hardly the best argument against golfing. The reason I have no difficulty in defending the idea of the humanities as an education for free people—free men and women—is that one of the great achievements of the modern world has been to establish a global consensus that we ought *all* to be free. In that sense—the central ideal of liberalism—that individuals are all entitled to lives of their own, lives in which the central, shaping decisions are for *them* to take and not to be settled for them by a master, is increasingly the common property of the species. If you doubt me, you have only to listen to the voices on the streets of Cairo, of Tunis, or Damascus; or read the impassioned essays of the Chinese political dissident, essayist, and poet Liu Xiaobo. And if you are to discharge the terrific responsibility of making your own—your only—life, then you surely need all the help you can get.

So why does an education in the humanities—an education *ad humanitatem*—provide part of the help you need? After all, you might think that what you actually need is to be found in the social and natural sciences. Psychology, especially the new, so-called positive psychology, and neuroscience can tell you what it takes for a normal person to achieve satisfaction; economics and political science help you think about what the effects of various public policies will be; physics and chemistry and biology tell us how the world works, so that we can take what we want from it. These things are all true.

But who is going to tell you what satisfactions are really worth pursuing? Which effects worth aiming for? What is worth wanting? Who will help you decide whether John Stuart Mill was right to say in *Utilitarianism,* "It is better to be a human being dissatisfied than a pig satisfied; better to be Socrates dissatisfied than a fool satisfied"?[13] Indeed, who will let you know this question is even worth asking? And where will you learn that one reason for studying the sciences is that understanding how the universe works, understanding where we fit into it, would be worthwhile in itself, even if we never put the knowledge to use in making a buck or winning a war?

The answer, I think, is evident. These are the questions you learn to face, learn to live with, learn, in the end, provisionally at least, to answer, with the help of literature and the arts, critically appreciated, through the study of philosophy and history and cultural anthropology.

I realize that saying these things, especially in sympathetic company, is liable to sound merely platitudinous. So let me make what I hope are less familiar points. The humanities are not just different from the sciences in providing us with a different kind of guidance in the making of our lives. They are different also, in several profound ways, in the character of their aims and methods.

Here are three such crucial distinctions. First, while generalizations—sonnets usually have fourteen lines—are important in the humanities, they are put to use in our studies in order to illuminate particular things: the universal in the humanities is in the service of the particular, to offer a formula. And this is because of the focus of so much humanistic work on individual artifacts: a particular poem, a particular painting, a particular sonata. Each is a worthy object of study, not just because it reveals something about poetry or painting or music, or, more generally, art or, more loftily yet, the human spirit, but because it is in itself worth explicating.

Natural scientists, on the other hand, are usually not interested *as scientists* in individual things—this atom or collection of molecules, this organism, this cell, this strand of DNA—but rather in the patterns they exemplify. Wilhelm Windelband, the nineteenth-century German philosopher, introduced a useful pair of terms for these different kinds of aims. He said those forms of knowledge that focus on the "historically specific" individual thing were *idiographic*—concerned with representing the particular. Others, he said, were driven by the *nomothetic* urge, the urge to discover laws or general patterns:

> So we can say: empirical disciplines are seeking through their experience of reality either the universal, in the form of a natural law, or the individual in a historically specific form. They consider, on the one side, the always-unchanging form, on the other, the unique, specific content, of what happens in reality. The first are law-based forms of knowledge, the others involve knowledge of particular events; the former teach what is eternally the case, the latter what once existed. Systematic knowledge is—if one may construct new terms of art—in the one case nomothetic, in the other idiographic.[14]

Windelband is insisting that both paying attention to individuals and looking for laws are part of the search for systematic knowledge of the world of experience: in fact, the word I translated as "empirical disciplines" just now was *Erfahrungswissenschaften*, which some would probably translate as "empirical sciences." So the Reverend White's *Natural History of Selborne*, though full of acute observations of the natural world surrounding an English village, is not a nomothetic work, though it contains reports that a scientist might have a use for. On November 4, 1767, Gilbert White wrote:

> As to the short-winged soft-billed birds, which come trooping in such numbers in the spring, I am at a loss even what to suspect about them. I watched them narrowly this year, and saw them abound till about Michaelmas, when they appeared no longer. Subsist they cannot openly among us, and yet elude the eyes of the inquisitive: and, as to their hiding, no man pretends to have found any of them in a torpid state in the winter. But with regard to their migration, what difficulties attend that supposition! that such feeble bad fliers (who

the summer long never flit but from hedge to hedge) should be able
to traverse vast seas and continents in order to enjoy milder seasons
amidst the regions of Africa![15]

For those with an idiographic interest, White's vision of the natural world
repays our attention, but so does Darwin's *Origin of Species*, even though
it is no longer by any stretch of the imagination the best scientific account
of its subject. For both of these books—one written as science, the other
composed before the word "biology" existed—offer up more than material for general conclusions.

This contrast between the humanist's broadly idiographic interests and
the nomothetic urges of the social and natural sciences is connected with
a second contrast, which has to do with the *point* of attention to those
particulars that concern us. Our aim is centrally to explicate—that is,
to account for the meaning, the significance, the symbolic working—of
those particulars. Narrative as a form of exegesis is one form of explication: we tell the story that explains the meaning. But explication has
other modes, as we know. One is the placing of a sign within a system of
rules: the formal rules that shape a poem, the grammatical rules that help
us interpret a difficult passage, and the like. Not any explication of any
humanly made thing is central to the project of the humanities. There are
too many particulars to be interested in all of them. We pick among them.
And—this is my third difference—we pick the ones that are significant for
certain kinds of human purpose.

Which human purposes? Well, unfortunately, human purposes evolve
and cannot be catalogued in advance. This is indeed one of the lessons
of the humanities. There is a well-known Latin tag that makes this point:
Tempora mutantur nos et mutamur in illis.[16] But whereas one *E. coli* will
do as well as another for biological study (as long as it has a genome of
the right kind), not any old pot or painting or verse is worthy of sustained
attention. There's an answer to the question why there are more essays on
Rembrandt's paintings than on Ruysdael's (accomplished as the latter no
doubt was); a reason why Mozart's works have received more attention
than Salieri's; a significance to the greater attention paid to Jane Austen
than to Walter Scott.

The third distinctive point about the humanities, then, is that the world
of the humanist is intrinsically tied up with the complex evaluations that
underlie these differentiated patterns of attention. And while bias of many

kinds—on account, for example, as we know too well, of class, nation, race, religion, and gender—and shifts of taste, from, say, Palladian classicism to Baroque elaboration, or from coldly abstract to messily political, are part of the history of the humanities, the point of what we do presupposes, I believe, that what we choose to teach and study is worth teaching because the understanding that is the product of our study enriches us as it enriches the lives of those to whom we pass it on. The result is that evaluation, judgment, discrimination in many dimensions are central to the practice of the humanities.

Once we see that the humanities are idiographic, attentive to explicating particulars, selected on the basis of a great diversity of human interests, requiring evaluations that are cognitive, emotional, aesthetic, moral, political, and social, this helps us to understand something about the forms of knowledge that they produce. A typical essay or treatise in the humanities doesn't proceed deductively, by stating first principles and drawing conclusions from them, or inductively, by assembling evidence for a general conclusion. It is instead allusive and associative: it places particular things—a poem, a philosophical argument, a painting, a pot, a movie—not only within the rules that help make them intelligible but also in the context of other particulars.

To explain what I mean here, let me repeat that Latin tag I just cited: *Tempora mutantur nos et mutamur in illis.* First, we will want to say what it means, by relying on the rules of the Latin language: *The times are changed, and we are changed in them.* The humanist will want to point out that this is probably not a classical formulation, even though it is in the classic hexameter of much Greek and Latin verse. The earliest version I know of, so far, is in Harrison's 1577 *Description of England*, in the third chapter, "Of the Laws of England," where he says it is "the saying of the Poet."[17] Harrison's *Description,* the humanist will probably also want you to know, was published as part of Raphael Holinshed's *Chronicles,* which were the major source for Shakespeare's material in his plays about the history of England; it is a collective work, in which Holinshed collaborated with Richard Stanyhurst, Edmund Campion— the Jesuit priest and martyr—and John Hooker. That "the saying" was regarded by Harrison as proverbial does not guarantee that it was of any great age: proverbs, after all, have to begin sometime. But he may have thought that it was, in fact, a line from a classical poem, since this is the age of the newly recovered classical humanism of the Renaissance.

This sort of allusive, associative placing of a cultural artifact—in this case a proverb in Latin verse—has a sort of shape that is now completely familiar to all of us. Why? Because it is the way we have come to contextualize items by following a series of hyperlinks on the World Wide Web. Indeed, so it seems to me, the form of knowledge on the web—assembled as much by linking one thing with another as by the content of any particular page—is, in some ways, the ideal form for the expression of humanistic knowledge, which consists, precisely, in being able to connect particulars as much as in placing them in the context of generalities. The hyperlink is the modern expression of the footnote—that great humanistic invention—but taken to its logical limit. (By the way, if you want to read a work by a great modern humanist, read Anthony Grafton's magisterial exploration *The Footnote: A Curious History*.)

Scientists and engineers and mathematicians have interests that are functional and goal-directed—or, as we philosophers say, teleological. They are driven by questions, and their knowledge consists in answers and a grasp of the tools for finding answers. For them, a footnote aims to point you to evidence or to fill in an argument. For us, what is in the footnotes is not out of the way; it is part of what we are after.

Now these are points about the forms of knowledge, not about the psychologies of the participants. There are no doubt humanists who think they are discovering universal truths; there are practitioners of literary theory and of ethics whose project this is. And there are scientists, like the great naturalist E. O. Wilson, who seem utterly taken up with, say, the lives of particular species of ants. So the claim I am making is about tendencies of thought, not an absolute division between the humanities and the sciences; and the central claim is that the association of particulars, bringing objects together, is an important form of knowledge, not mere rambling.

Let me return now, as I promised, to Hazlitt. Hazlitt's recognition that the arts were not progressive is right, I believe, because the lessons of the arts, like the lessons of the humanities, are, as he says, not "reducible to rule or capable of demonstration." What he noticed was that among the particulars worthy of our present attention, among the objects worth passing on, are many from remote times, while the scientific theory of remote times was of no contemporary scientific interest, because science is interested in the general—what is reducible to rule—and what can be demonstrated. But, of course, ancient science can be an object of humanistic study, because we can be interested in those ancient theories in the way in which we are interested in ancient art and ancient literature: because an understanding of them enriches us now, whether or not the theories still hold our attention as guides to the nature of reality. That is why Locke and Freud and Goethe are of continuing humanistic interest. If you were driven by the nomothetic urge, you would say that these theories were of interest because of what they tell us about the human mind that produced them. But the truth is that most of what we learn about the human mind, in a general way, from the study of old medical or psychological or biological theories, could be learned from the study of contemporary mentalities. If you are in the nomothetic mode, one theory (like one *E. coli* colony) will do just as well as another.

What we have to accept, I think, as one of the key differences between the humanities and the sciences, is, as I have suggested, that our practice is based in the faith that it is worth passing on an understanding of the intellectual, literary, and artistic practices of our predecessors, even when their theories have been shown to be scientifically untenable, even when we have no interest in reproducing their arts or their poems. We pass them on because without this knowledge, the objects worth attending to are not intelligible, cannot be explicated, absorbed, responded to, in the ways that matter. It is a wonderful thing to be able to communicate the power, intelligence, and pathos of a Horatian ode—including the pathos of the fact that he was right when he wrote "Exegi monumentum aere perennius,"[18] for the bronze memorials of his day are indeed few and far between and yet we still have every one of his "carmina," as he called them, his songs; but the writing of a new ode in Horatian style would be a mere curiosity.

What this means for the future of the humanities, thus understood, is simple enough. Unlike the nomothetes, we will always be holding onto the past, because we have faith not just that much of what was done in the past is worth understanding for its own sake—not because it explains the present, nor because it illuminates the universal, and because it is worth understanding, worth knowing, it is worth passing on. Ethics in the hands of philosophers like myself, among others, teaches us that a worthwhile life has to contain things worth doing; but that one thing worth doing is attending to these artifacts is a lesson learned by anyone who has been well taught in the humanities. The humanities are intrinsically connected with teaching: to make these objects intelligible, we must teach their contexts, their systems of significance, the rules and the rule-breaking that made them. That is what makes them capable of explication. Our study of them is connected with the need to understand them, but the need to understand them depends on the conviction that they are worth holding onto and passing on.

Science does at least two kinds of work for us: it delivers understanding and it allows us technological progress (and technological peril). That understanding—of the laws of our world—is, like humanistic understanding, a thing of intrinsic value, something worth having, even if it did not deliver the technological payoff. You are enriched by understanding the best contemporary scientific picture of the world, but you can be grateful to the scientists even if you don't know that story, because of the great technological yield of modern science. Of course, the humanities have utilitarian benefits, too: well-trained English literature majors write better memos and movie scripts than most badly trained ones, and certainly than those who have not learned to read deeply and well. And the theory and practice of composition play a central role in producing a society that communicates and creates with power and efficiency.

But the rest of what we humanists do lives or dies—unlike the work of the sciences—by whether we communicate what we do to each generation of students, persuading them that these particulars whose understanding we profess are worthy objects of their contemporary attention. They can be persuaded—I was going to say they can easily be persuaded, but alas, I am not sure that is true—that some of the music and movies and television of our own era are worth attending to, and, once persuaded, of this, it is not too hard to show them that this requires more than merely passively absorbing them. And many of these present objects do, indeed, draw out humanistic attention in exactly the way that an ode of Horace or an illuminated manuscript or a chorale by Purcell might do. But it is harder to persuade many of them of the virtues of these older objects. My own view, as I hope I have made plain, is that persuading them of this is an essential part of the vocation of the humanist. We must speak to non-specialists because we must speak to the untrained young. If our faith is warranted, then what we have to offer them is something to take on into their lives beyond college.

This is, perhaps, an old-fashioned way of thinking of what we are doing. But the hope of the humanist is, in my view, essentially that there is so much from the past to pass on. I am all for new methods, as I hope

I have also made clear. But they are in the service of a mission that is as old as formal education: to provide each new generation with the frameworks of understanding that will allow them to interpret a significant number of the many particulars that are our human heritage. That significant number is, as a moment's reflection reminds us, a diminishing proportion of what there is to explicate. When I was an undergraduate, a teacher—actually a biochemistry teacher—gave me a chromolithograph of one of Carpaccio's great murals, the one called the *Vision of St. Jerome*. It's called this even though it's a picture of St. Augustine, because it's *his* vision of the older saint that is pictured. Years later, looking at the original painting for the first time in Venice, it struck me that the shelf of books behind the saint—his library—contained most of the books that he would have thought worth reading, and that he would almost certainly have read all of them. When the scriptorium was replaced by the printing press, one of the limiting steps in the proliferation of writing was almost removed; when the internet became available, the barriers came down completely. Now, each week in California, thousands of times the number of pages that St. Augustine could have read in his lifetime are published on paper, millions of times that number on the web. Once, to hear the range of music that I can scan in a few minutes on my car radio, I would have had to have traveled thousands of miles and been lucky to arrive for the right performances. The DVDs in my own house (leave aside the films I can access through the web) contain more hours of human acting than Samuel Pepys (1633–1703) or John Aubrey (1626–1697)—devoted theatergoers both—ever saw in their entire lives. We are, in short, drowning in the particulars we humanists study.

Surely, now, in such a time, it is more urgent than ever to speak for what is most rewarding in this great flood of artifacts, so that those whom we can persuade to care for the magnificent particulars will spend the little time each of us has to attend to them well. (We will also want to convey the many virtues of minor works and the need, if we are to understand excellence, for a familiarity with some of what is ordinary.) In this time, more than in any earlier time, the civilization we live in needs the work of the humanist. If the evidence is, increasingly, that our fellow citizens doubt this, that is our fault, not theirs, for teaching this need and then responding to it is our vocation and our task.

There are extraordinary new tools for that project available to us now. When I sat down to write this essay, I had P. P. Howe's edition of the works of Hazlitt to hand, because it is part of our library at home; you, however, do not need to acquire this rare commodity because most of Hazlitt is somewhere on the web. I could check on the Latin prose and verse that I half remember from my youth because of the Perseus website, from which I got not just the texts but also the dictionaries and the cross-references for thinking about them. You can read those almost anywhere on the planet. We have so much more to read, yes, but we also have—and we need to develop—more tools for finding things to read, more, in the jargon, metadata that help us scan the terabytes for the kilobyte we need now.

One other thing we need is a richer store of materials in other traditions—more texts in Africa's hundreds of languages, for example, along with the dictionaries and grammars for those who do not speak them to begin to make sense of them.[19] If you wanted to know why they should be there, I should direct you to one of the sententiae left to us from the plays of Terence, P. Terentius Afer, the African, the Roman comedian of Berber ancestry: a line that Michel de Montaigne helped make famous later by inscribing it on the beams of his study in the sixteenth century: *Homo sum, humani a me nihil alienum puto.* It doesn't matter that in the *Self-Tormentor*, the play from which this line comes, it is actually an invocation of the right to interfere in the affairs of your neighbor. It has become one of the great cosmopolitan slogans of humanism. And when I started thinking about the ethical significance of our now ever more global society some years ago, it was an even older figure—Diogenes of Sinope, the first cosmopolitan, the first person to make a philosophy based on the idea that he was a citizen of the world—who set me on the way.

But if it's the particulars that are our distinctive contribution, let me exemplify their power finally in a single writer, one I just mentioned. In February 1571, on his thirty-eighth birthday, a one-time lawyer and courtier had a Latin inscription incised on a beam in his study: "Worn out with the slavery of the court and of public service, Michel de Montaigne . . . retires to the bosom of the learned Muses . . . to pass what may be left of a life already more than half spent, consecrating this ancestral dwelling and sweet retreat to his liberty, tranquility and repose."[20] Saul Frampton, in a wonderful recent book on Montaigne, describes how other "classical and biblical quotations curled across the joists and beams of his ceiling, like vines around the branches of a tree."[21] Latin for Montaigne wasn't just the language of the new Renaissance humanism; it was effectively his mother tongue. His father—himself only a generation removed from the trade in wine, fish, and plant dyes that had made the family rich enough to acquire the estate at Montaigne—had decided that little Micheau should be raised as a proper aristocrat. He hired a learned tutor from Germany and commanded him to speak to the boy only in Latin. Even the servants were required to do so. As a result, Montaigne wrote later, he was over six before he understood "any more French or Périgordian than Arabic."[22]

But the plan on his thirty-eighth birthday was to hunker down at the Dordogne chateau where he grew up, situated on the edge of hills that stretched northward toward Limousin. The sweetest part of the retreat, for him, was his library, vast for its time, of about a thousand books. Soon he began to write the short prose pieces in French that he was to call his *essais*.

In the French of Montaigne's day, we should recall, the word *essai* meant something assayed or essayed: an experiment, a tasting. Certainly there had never been anything in literature like these essays before; the experiment paid off—it tasted good. But it was a pretty strange experiment. One essay, "On Some Verses from Virgil," begins with the annoyances of aging. Many pages in, he announces his theme: "What has the act of generation done to men (an action so natural, so necessary, and so just) that we dare not speak of it without shame?"[23] That leads us, via the Virgil passage, which is about marital sex between Venus and Vulcan, to a discussion of sex and marriage generally. Before long, he is bemoaning the inadequacy of his own endowment. Montaigne ends what he himself calls "a stream of babble" by remarking that men and women are "cast in the same mold," except for what is due to "education and customs."[24] The essay is about as linear as a series of blog posts.

In a preface to his collection, "To the Reader," Montaigne warns us that he has only a personal aim: to leave behind a sketch of his character. He's interested neither in any service to the rest of us nor in any glory for himself. "So, reader," he concludes, "I am myself the matter of my book: that is no reason for you to employ your leisure on a subject so frivolous and so vain. Farewell, then."[25] Montaigne greets us with a farewell only because he knows that we will be unable to resist the temptation to turn the page and read on.

Montaigne knows he tends to free-associate: one of his most frequent tics is to say some version of "Let me get back to the subject." In the essay "Of Books," he demands that an author "begin with the main point."[26] It was a

standard he never once met himself. If the humanist's knowledge is made up
in large measure of allusion and association, he owes us no apology.

As an essayist, he preferred to capture consciousness via an artful sort
of interior monologue. But the essays do have a certain consistency of
outlook, and Montaigne's perspective was as novel as his style. In fact,
he has a fair claim to being the first liberal. (We could say the first liberal,
then, was almost a Limousin liberal.)

Liberalism, as I said earlier, has at its heart the idea of the free man
and woman. What's important, liberalism holds, to put it the other way
round, is whatever is important about not being unfree, not being a slave.
I suggested that one thing that matters is being in charge of the making
of your own life; in the spirit of John Stuart Mill, we could call that indi-
viduality. The individual is not a slave to a master, but also not a slave to
a government and not a slave to public opinion. Mill, you'll recall, worried that "the opinions of masses of merely average men are everywhere
become or becoming the dominant power,"[27] and he wanted us to resist
this tendency. So liberalism has both the doctrine that all people should
be free and an interpretation of what freedom is and why it matters. But
it also has, at its core, some dispositions, some habits of mind, and principally these two: an abhorrence of cruelty and a sense of the provisional
nature of human knowledge. These tendencies of thought are everywhere
evident in Montaigne's sensibility.

To see how distinctive it was, it helps to recall the times. He was sur-
rounded by religious strife that raged throughout his adult life, including
the infamous Massacre of St. Bartholomew, in which thousands (or
perhaps tens of thousands—no one knows exactly how many) were mas-
sacred in Paris and the provinces.

So Montaigne was urging toleration at a time when you could be
burned at the stake for an error in theology. "It's putting one's conjectures
at quite a high price, to burn a living man for them," he wryly observed in
the essay "On the Lame," taking aim, in a single shot, at overconfidence
and at cruelty, which he termed the "ultimate of the vices."[28] Judith Shklar,
the great theorist of liberalism, has suggested why the two are more than
contingently related. To hold cruelty to be the first of vices, she says, is to
turn from the way revealed religion understands sin—as offenses against
God. That's easier if you can entertain the possibility that your religious
convictions are wrong. Cruelty, Shklar says, is "a purely human verdict
upon human conduct, and so puts religion at a certain distance."[29]

These aspects of Montaigne's temperament—his resistance to cruelty and his fallibilism—are ones from which we can still learn. They are liberal because they are part of the temperamental equipment of a free man who aims to live at peace among a free people. We learn these things well from Montaigne because the way in which he teaches combines, in Jonathan Swift's old metaphor, sweetness with light. He coaxes, I would almost say seduces us into his vision. The particulars of the *Essays* are worth attending to in their own right, but that is not to deny, as I have also insisted, that coming to know them has many other advantages. These powerful lessons about the best way for men and women to live together as free people are among the benefits.

But the reasons why the particulars are worth attending to, and the consequential benefits of that attention, are not just one; they are many. That is why the case for the humanities is not one- but many-stranded, and it is learned best by doing what we do: attending to those diverse things we claim command the disparate forms of human attention.

Notes

1. Hazlitt, "Shakespeare and Milton," 44.
2. "The publisher and drawing master Rudolf Ackermann (1764–1834), had come to London from Germany in his early twenties. A philanthropist and businessman, the money he raised to help Leipzig after its devastation by Napoleon in 1813 made him a public figure in both England and Germany. The *Microcosm of London*, which combined the comic genius (although kept on a tight leash by Ackermann) of Thomas Rowlandson who executed the figures and the precise architectural draughtsmanship of Augustus Pugin, was intended to provide an intimate look at the major buildings and landmarks of Georgian London." Michael Finney Antique Books and Print, "The Microcosm of London."
3. Hazlitt, "Why the Arts Are Not Progressive?," 160–64.
4. Hazlitt, "Shakespeare," 44–45.
5. *Quarterly Review*, 424–25. For the attribution to Barrett see Cutmore, "Quarterly Review Archive," 487, article 9.
6. The legal issues in the case are discussed in Husband, "The Prosecution of Archias." But, of course, *Pro Archia* is best known now for the defense of poetry.
7. "Nam ut primum ex pueris excessit Archias, atque ab eis artibus quibus aetas puerilis ad humanitatem informari solet se ad scribendi studium contulit, primum Antiochiae—nam ibi natus est loco nobili—celebri quondam urbe et copiosa, atque eruditissimis hominibus liberalissimisque studiis adfluenti, celeriter antecellere omnibus ingeni gloria contigit." Cicero, "M. Tvlli Ciceronis Pro A. Licinio Archia Poeta Oratio," para. 4.

8. "Etenim omnes artes, quae ad humanitatem pertinent, habent quoddam commune vinculum, et quasi cognatione quadam inter se continentur." Ibid., para. 2.

9. "Hoc concursu hominum literatissimorum, hac vestra humanitate . . . patiamini de studiis humanitatis ac litterarum paulo loqui liberius." Ibid., para. 3.

10. "Sit igitur, judices, sanctum apud vos, humanissimos homines, hoc poetae nomen, quod nulla umquam barbaria violavit." Ibid., para. 19.

11. See the Latin Word Study Tool, "Humanitas."

12. They go on to specify that *liberalis* can mean "gentlemanly, noble, noble-minded, honorable, ingenuous, gracious, kind." See the Latin Word Study Tool, "Studium."

13. Mill, "Chapter 2."

14. In his essay "Geschichte und Naturwissenschaft," Windelband wrote, "So dürfen wir sagen: die Erfahrungswissenschaften suchen in der Erkenntnis des Wirklichen entweder das Allgemeine in der Form des Naturgesetzes oder *das Einzelne* in der geschichtlich bestimmten Gestalt; sie betrachten zu einem Teil die immer sich gleichbleibende Form, zum anderen Teil den einmaligen, in sich bestimmten Inhalt des wirklichen Geschehens. Die einen sind Gesetzeswissenschaften, die anderen Ereigniswissenschaften; jene lehren, was immer ist, diese, was einmal war. Das wissenschaftliche Denken ist—wenn man neue Kunstausdrücke bilden darf—in dem einen Falle *nomothetisch*, in dem andern idiographisch."

15. White, *The Natural History of Selborne*, 33.

16. I learned of this source from Wikipedia, which doesn't, however, get it quite right. But that's okay because you can find a version of the original Holinshed on the web.

17. Harrison, *The Description of England*, 99.

18. "I have completed a monument more enduring than bronze." Horace, *Carmina*, III.30.

19. So I am proud to have contributed to this task, along with my mother and a colleague, by publishing *Bu Me Be: Proverbs of the Akan*.

20. Frampton, *When I Am Playing*, 4.

21. Ibid., 1.

22. Ibid., 20.

23. "Qu'a faict l'action genitale aux hommes, si naturelle, si necessaire et si juste, pour n'en oser parler sans vergongne."

24. "Ce notable commentaire, qui m'est eschappé d'un flux de caquet," "je dis que les masles et femelles sont jettez en mesme moule: sauf l'institution et l'usage, la difference n'y est pas grande."

25. "Ainsi, lecteur, je suis moy-mesmes la matiere de mon livre: ce n'est pas raison que tu employes ton loisir en un subject si frivole et si vain. A Dieu donq, de Montaigne, ce premier de Mars mille cinq cens quatre vingts."

26. "Je veux qu'on commence par le dernier point."

27. Mill, *Collected Works*, 269.

28. "Apres tout, c'est mettre ses conjectures à bien haut pris que d'en faire cuire un homme tout vif."

29. Shklar, *Ordinary Vices*, 9.

Works Cited

Appiah, Peggy, Kwame Anthony Appiah, and Ivor Agyeman-Duah. *Bu Me Be: Proverbs of the Akan*. Banbury, Oxon, U.K.: Ayebia Clarke, 2007.

Bourdieu, Pierre. *Distinction: A Social Critique of the Judgment of Taste*. Cambridge, Mass.: Harvard University Press, 1987.

Cicero. "M. Tvlli Ciceronis Pro A. Licinio Archia Poeta Oratio." Latin Library. Accessed June 20, 2018. http://www.thelatinlibrary.com/cicero/arch.shtml.

Cutmore, Jonathan ed. "Quarterly Review Archive." *Romantic Circles*. Accessed June 20, 2018. http://www.rc.umd.edu/reference/qr/index/38.html.

Frampton, Saul. *When I Am Playing with My Cat How Do I Know That She Is Not Playing with Me? Montaigne and Being in Touch with Life*. New York: Pantheon, 2011.

Grafton, Anthony. *The Footnote: A Curious History*. Cambridge, Mass.: Harvard University Press, 1999.

Harrison, William. *The Description of England*. University of Oxford, Faculty of English. Accessed June 20, 2018. http://english.nsms.ox.ac.uk/holinshed/texts.php?text1=1577_0080.

Hazlitt, William. "Shakespeare and Milton." In *The Complete Works of William Hazlitt*, edited by P. P. Howe, vol. 5. London: J. M. Dent & Sons, 1930.

———. "Why the Arts Are Not Progressive?—A Fragment." In *The Complete Works of William Hazlitt*, edited by P. P. Howe, vol. 4. London: J. M. Dent & Sons, 1930.

Husband, Richard Wellington. "The Prosecution of Archias." *Classical Journal* 9, no. 4 (1914): 165–71.

Latin Word Study Tool. "Humanitas." Accessed June 20, 2018. http://www.perseus.tufts.edu/hopper/morph?l=humanitas&la=la#lexicon.

———. "Studium." Accessed June 20, 2018. http://www.perseus.tufts.edu/hopper/morph?l=studium&la=la#lexicon.

Michael Finney Antique Books and Print. "The Microcosm of London. Surrey Institution." Accessed June 20, 2018. http://www.michaelfinney.co.uk/catalogue/category/item/index.cfm?asset_id=2887.

Mill, John Stuart. "Chapter 2: What Utilitarianism Is." In *The Collected Works of John Stuart Mill*. Vol. 10: *Essays on Ethics, Religion, and Society*, edited by John M. Robson. Toronto: University of Toronto Press, Routledge and Kegan Paul, 1985. Accessed June 20, 2018. http://oll.libertyfund.org/title/241/21504/762298.

———. *The Collected Works of John Stuart Mill*. Vol. 18: *Essays on Politics and Society, Part I (On Liberty)*, edited by John M. Robson. Toronto: University of Toronto Press, Routledge and Kegan Paul, 1985.

Montaigne, Michel de. "Au lecteur" [To the reader]. *Les Essais I. The Montaigne Project*. Accessed June 20, 2018. http://artflsrv02.uchicago.edu/cgi-bin/philologic/getobject.pl?c.0:2:0.montaigne.

———. "De L'institution des enfans" [On the education of children]. *Les Essais I. 26. The Montaigne Project*. Accessed June 20, 2018. http://artflsrv02.uchicago.edu/cgi-bin/philologic/getobject.pl?c.0:2:26.montaigne.

———. "Des Boyteux" [On the lame]. *Les Essais III. 11. The Montaigne Project*. Accessed June 20, 2018. http://artflsrv02.uchicago.edu/cgi-bin/philologic/getobject.pl?c.0:4:10.montaigne.

———. "Des Livres" [Of books]. *Les Essais II. 10. The Montaigne Project*. Accessed June 20, 2018. http://artflsrv02.uchicago.edu/cgi-bin/philologic/getobject.pl?c.0:3:9.montaigne.

———. "Sur des vers de Virgile" [On some verses from Virgil]. *Les Essais III. 5. The Montaigne Project*. Accessed June 20, 2018. http://artflsrv02.uchicago.edu/cgi-bin/philologic/getobject.pl?c.0:4:4.montaigne.

Quarterly Review 19, no. 38 (1818): 424–25. http://spenserians.cath.vt.edu/TextRecord.php?action=GET&textsid=36138.

Shklar, Judith. *Ordinary Vices*. Cambridge, Mass.: Harvard University Press, 1984.

White, Gilbert. *The Natural History of Selborne*. Project Gutenberg. Accessed June 18, 2018. http://www.gutenberg.org/ebooks/1408.

Windelband, Wilhelm. "Geschichte und Naturwissenschaft." Straßburger Rektoratsrede in *Präludien, Aufsätze und Reden zur Philosophie und ihrer Geschichte*, 136–60. Tubingen: J. C. B. Mohr, 1894.

Uberizing the University

David Theo Goldberg

Over nearly two decades now, and across the globe, the university has been undergoing profound changes.[1] The processes and pressures prompting these shifts have been uneven, if more or less incessant. For much of the twentieth century, and especially after World War II, the university served as the vehicle of upward mobility, the principal pathway to securing middle-class and eventually upper-middle-class life. Obviously this has been checkered across types of institutions of higher learning. Elite private universities, especially prior to the 1940s, quite explicitly maintained and sustained privilege, seeking increasingly since then to lift a small slither of the disprivileged into elevated status. Public universities were founded on the mission to offer pathways into middle-class life, while community colleges served first in the role technical schools have done in other countries and more recently as pathways to public four-year institutions.

This prevailing twentieth-century model of the university began to give way in the later 1980s, slowly at first, then more dramatically and visibly with the onset of the new millennium. In the U.S. increasingly conservative and vocal legislatures in states such as Arizona began questioning the use of public funds by state universities for specific courses, programs, and hires. Once the investment in a reliably upwardly middle-class life for millions, by the new millennium higher education was no longer a presumptive public good. The stagnation in middle-class wages materialized alongside the mounting attack on affirmative action admission and hiring. Recessionary budgeting signaled deeper and deeper cuts to public universities, starting the downward spiral of public funding for higher education from the mid-1990s on. One recession after another—1993–95, 2002–4, 2008 on—only served to deepen and accelerate the shifts. Donald Trump's election to the U.S. presidency is as much the effect as the deepening of these shifts.

The percentage of university budgets provided by states is instructive. The University of California system exemplifies what happened earlier in Michigan and Virginia, and later across virtually all state systems around the country. In 2000 California provided about 27 percent of a $15 billion annual university system budget. By 2010, following two recessions, it was down to roughly 15 percent of nearly $20 billion. Today it hovers around 12 percent of $27 billion. Since 1960 the University of Michigan has seen approximately an 80 percent drop in state support, which now makes up a little more than 4 percent of its total annual revenue.[2] The University of Virginia receives less than 6 percent of its total funding from the state. Comparable, if locally specific, trends now face universities in Britain and Europe, Australia and South Africa, among others.

These trends have been fueled by the drive to privatize what were once public goods. The ideological "imperative" of austerity, the demonization of the university as the bastion of liberal values, the elevation of centralizing administration and board oversight at the expense of faculty governance, and the centering of professions and work preparation (STEM, technology, business, and law) as the dominant, if not singular, goal of higher education, while disparaging the human sciences and the arts, have profoundly transformed how the university is understood, as well as how it conceives and organizes itself. Politicians have earned cheap, ill-informed, and misdirecting points by insisting that "unemployable" degrees in the likes of English or anthropology no longer receive state support. These trends toward skillification at the expense of critical thinking, gathering steam since the 1980s, have only intensified with the Trump administration, which has hypercharged longer-standing attempts to defund completely the National Endowment for the Humanities and National Endowment for the Arts.

Revenue shortfalls from state budget cuts have been made up largely by significantly increased fees, from a rising percentage of out-of-state and international students, from renewed cuts, and from a range of newly creative revenue streams. The urge to admit more nonstate and foreign students is driven by the fact that they generally pay twice the fee rates of local students. From 2001 to 2013 nationwide state contributions to public research universities halved, while student fees nearly doubled.[3] The doubling of fees has also contributed significantly to spiraling student debt and the slowing number of less wealthy attendees at flagship state schools, despite the schools' best attempts to compete with well-endowed private colleges to provide significant financial aid.

These structural changes underpin an emergent "philosophy" of the new university today, which should prompt anyone concerned about the direction of higher education to pause. It is perhaps completely understandable that higher education would be fiscally impacted by and adapt to trying economic conditions more generally. But the extent and nature of the cuts are utterly shortsighted. Chris Newfield and Michael Meranze calculate that in California public universities could be fully funded at an annual average per person tax increase of just $48.[4] This would represent an investment in both a more thoroughly educated and productive workforce and a more engaged body of citizens. What is more disturbing than the economic and civic blinkers, however, is the way the fiscal challenges have been tied to a radically new and largely implicit, let alone thoroughly untested, conception of what and who the university is for and how it should be run.

Increasingly universities have been reorganized to privilege revenue-generating ventures and to restructure themselves along contemporary corporate lines. The rate of administrative staffing, planning, and oversight has far outstripped academic faculty hires and intellectual imperatives and appointments. Faculty governance is being largely hollowed out, replaced with top-down organizational mandates with less and less substantive faculty consultation. The logics of accounting and audit culture have assumed a central place of organizational purpose.

At the same time, administrative functionality on the ground has shifted more and more to the shoulders of individual faculty and their departments, as too have an increasing proportion of the ordinary operational costs. Room rentals, cleaning, and after-hours heating or air-conditioning or in some cases increased bandwidth all come with a fee structure to be borne by the academic units initiating the requests. Faculty phone lines have been cut in the interests of savings, relying instead on personal cell phone accounts. Mandatory campus closures—for example, over end-of-the-year breaks—have become a matter of course. In short, units and individuals are being made responsible for covering the costs of their own infrastructural needs.

In this shifting academic landscape, entrepreneurialism has tended to outrun critical pushback. As critical voices are being sidelined and in some cases completely suppressed, grant-seeking, consultancy work, spin-off start-ups, and corporate ventures have become the driving logic supporting and supplementing academic work, costs, and even salaries. Indirect cost recovery has become an increasingly significant proportion of annual university budgeting both institutionally and individually (in the latter instance, in addition to paying for the research and to cover graduate student and postdoctoral support, also to cover operating and material costs: phones, computers, academic staff support, etc.). Entrepreneurial faculty spin off profit-seeking companies and consultancies, in some cases developing lucrative businesses. Perhaps the most visible examples in the past few years have been the massive open online course ventures Udacity and Coursera, both spun off by Stanford faculty, but they are far from alone.

This logic of faculty enterprise impacts undergraduate teaching also, now disproportionately done by adjunct or contingent instructors. Contingent faculty (including adjuncts) have increased from 43 percent of the teaching force in 1975 to just over 70 percent today.[5] Undergraduate—and especially lower-division—courses are being disproportionately taught by instructors with no job security or standing in the university. Adjuncts are the temp workers of the academy. They have little voice, are paid less than it is possible to live on, and tend to have no benefits. They enable universities to cover basic courses at very low cost, with little if any obligation to the shadow workforce. As a consequence, they are less likely than tenured faculty to speak out and more likely to favor teaching conventional subject matter and approaches over more controversial or experimental ones. And in many cases, these "road scholars," named for driving the highway between many employing campuses on a given day, are unlikely over time to enjoy the conditions to sustain state-of-the-art expertise in a field. They may be teaching in areas of their discipline about which they have relatively less knowledge.

The growing erosion of tenure at major universities, as represented most notably by the Wisconsin university system, along with irregular salary increases and dwindling research support from within public institutions, suggest the creeping "casualization" of work conditions for ladder-rank faculty too. This has gone hand in glove with spiraling competition for both research funding and tenure-track positions; a recent open search on my campus in a highly ranked traditional social science department produced over four hundred applications for a single appointment. This has become quite standard. And faculty constantly feel they are under surveillance—by administrators and legislators, political lobby groups and issue advocates, as well as students and their parents. Morale has sunk like cement in water.

There are significant impacts too, as a consequence, on the learning side of the equation. As students increasingly stress certification and job placement, learning institutions are responding with highlighting the college "experience," as much socially as intellectually. The social experience—dorm living, recreational and social networking opportunities—has spiraled in selection and review importance as tuition costs have more than doubled. There has been a move to personal preference and interest learning—more often than not a function of perceived marketability—at a cost to a common body of knowledge and plain old fascination. This is not to deny that both are important, but the former is eclipsing the latter with growing alacrity.

Taken together, then, these trends amount to "uberizing" the university. How so? "Uber," broadly conceived, represents on-demand access, a claim to a flawless experience with minimized hassle, no commitment, and immediate gratification, all at the best going rates. It provides the digital platform drawing together the elements necessary for instant delivery, while passing along—one could say passing *down*—and hiding from view some of the significant delivery costs, such as for maintenance and operations, health care and social security. So the "Uberversity" provides to larger or lesser extent a platform and experience rather than the foundation for lifelong learning, conceptual and critical thinking, methodological and analytic rigor, listening and clarity, coherent argumentation and engagement.[6] The Uberversity—the uberized university—privileges in-time on-demand vocational skilling for the task at hand rather than the capacity for deep thinking. It increasingly turns to data-driven managerial imperatives. This means fewer opportunities to interact with managers for thoughtful discussion and feedback about one's workfare. "Operators"—whether drivers, teachers, or administrative staff—are considered not employees but service providers and are managed through monitoring and rating systems in semi-automated loops of big data and messaging.

Just as one can follow in real time on the platform map the progress of the Uber cab approaching the pickup point, so one can map out and monitor the timeline of working through the training modules for which the student has registered. Faculty too are being subjected to mandated "trainings" regarding sexual harassment, inventory handling, or, where applicable, for supervisory directions and regulations. Broken into modulated sessions, the platform regulates the minimal amount of standardized time to be spent on each module, mapping progress through the learning session. But the system also entails that "clients" or "customers"—the new learner, the uberlearner—are being "mapped" to ensure one is spending the minimal time necessary to complete the lessons offered. This has become, in effect, the learning ankle bracelet, the surveillance sensor. While there are test questions to complete each module, there is no passing or failing. All this means, in principle, that instructors could be monitored for the time they take both to prepare and oversee online learning modules, and students can get certificated (now digitally "badged") with no assurance they have learned anything. The certification autogenerated by the platform, much like the Uber receipt on one's smartphone, is more about customer service, liability, and immunity from potential litigation than it is about consequential knowledge acquisition.

In effect, Uber represents the "unbundling" of the elements traditionally making up the conduct of business. The Uber platform, its operation and administration, are delinked from the service provision with which it is associated. Uber, its spokespeople invariably insist, is a "platform" for ordering a ride. It does not own the cars providing rides (at least not yet, as the company has been experimenting on developing driverless cars). It bears none of the latter service costs, from maintenance of vehicles to driver costs (though the latter, of course, have now been challenged in court). The university too has moved expeditiously in recent years to unbundle. Knowledge provision—the academic mission—has been cut off from services and counseling, each department running discretely and semi-autonomously, challenged to cover its own costs in a per unit pay-to-play or plug-in configuration. Professional and recreational networks enabled by the academic institution have little if anything to do with each other. They are value-added attractions at best, driving determination of the institution in its most extreme cases.

Similarly the current culture of crowdsourcing is upending traditional modes of assessment. Uber accompanies the electronic ride receipt with a persistent request for ride evaluation: one can check the rating of one's assigned driver as the car approaches. Analogously real-time teaching evaluations are becoming the new mode of review. A growing number of campuses are introducing a clicker system for in-class student assessment of the lecture in progress. Much like CNN voter-viewer ratings of political debates in process, the system registers student ratings of a lecture module as boring or interesting, informative or obtuse, indicating the ratings for all to see on the screen behind the lecturer. The aim (so the rationalization goes) is for the instructor to adjust immediately within the class in progress to the students' thumbs up or rotten tomatoes. RateMyProfessors.com is so yesterday!

This reduction to purely transactional economies has a series of ripple effects. The university aspires to a brand and to becoming a branding institution. The perceived value of the brand underwrites the price of the certificate awarded. Ranking, of the student experience and the major college sports teams at least as much as the academic function, becomes the driving logic of institutional life and reputational capital. Some knowledges consequently get occluded, to the point first of irrelevance and then ultimately nonrecognition even as valuable. In undergraduate physics courses today, for example, conceptual thinking key to advancing knowledge in the field and once central to learning physics has largely disappeared. It has been replaced by heightened training in the technical and mathematical skills necessary to the discipline. Rote over reasoning.

Uber U. faculty, where necessary at all, amount to brokers in the knowledge economy, hedge fund managers whose function is to network students to those marketplace skills, services, and social competencies necessary to get ahead. Already mini-administrators, they are now also entrepreneurs. Much of the base-level training—what should be foundational—is outsourced to adjuncts who are expected likewise to bear all of the self-sustaining and reproducing costs. As these costs are downstreamed onto less resourced and unprotected individuals and the university units they occupy, so too is responsibility for any misdirection, wrongdoing, or failure. The institution washes its hands of any malfunctioning agent, the marginalized bad apple or malperforming program.

As state support for public education has diminished in the drive to its uberizing, extra- and intra-institutional surveillance has ramped up. Externally, state legislatures, agencies, and politically minded prosecutors have attended more closely to academic activities. Legislatures have targeted what they consider politically progressive courses or unemployable degrees across the humanities and social sciences, threatening defunding. Prosecutors have picked on speech they consider politically disruptive or unacceptable. Even political lobby groups and critics have tried to constrain speech or activities on campus they deem disagreeable. They proceed by issuing frequent Freedom of Information Act requests or Title VI accusations to the Civil Rights Division of the Department of Education to curtail the targeted campus organizations or individuals. And more extremely, organizations funded by the likes of David Horowitz or Sheldon Adelson have established faculty and student watch lists of those at odds with their own political commitments.

Internally, institutional administrations have focused attention on faculty and students they believe pose liabilities to the institutional brand or fundraising capacity. More generally, university administrations have heightened oversight of fiscal and reputational considerations of academic units. Audit culture and fear have ballooned; assessment and rating regimes have become paramount; mandatory online training modules have proliferated. Students have become customers, their paying parents investors with nominal voting—and by extension unstated veto—power. Such considerations too are driving the corporatizing culture of higher education today.

These are currently trending directions across the academy. As we know from social media, trends are fickle and can shift quickly at any moment. They are disproportionately and incompletely in play across a broad range of institutions, restructuring some more deeply than others. But they are deeply at work reshaping social, political, and so institutional priorities and dispositions. As with Uber, taken discretely rather than systemically, these developments in some respects respond to existing needs while also unsettling sedimented and often outmoded structures. Just as the Uber platform makes getting a ride easier, often less expensive, easily shareable, and cashless, so the Uberversity platform potentially simplifies getting credentialed and is supposed (improbably) to drive down costs and render higher learning more accessible. These new developments no doubt can challenge us to think anew about higher education, opening up creative opportunities to refashion pedagogical and operating practices, advance student learning, and transform knowledge production across a broad swath of areas.

For example, just as Uber individualizes the ride experience in some particular ways, so there is an emerging trend to individualize academic degrees. Uber rides are not hailed on the street, as regular cabs are. They are ordered on the Uber platform, supposedly arriving within minutes (though the minutes to ride arrival specified on the platform tend not to be New York minutes but long, strung out ones). The ride cost calculation varies not simply by the relation of distance and time but also by car demand and supply at the specified time. Universities similarly have taken, to some extent, to offering nano-degrees. These are hyperspecified degrees tailored to individually desired skill sets. No general distribution or qualifying requirements, no writing or critical thinking courses. No student cohort and consequently little if any peer-to-peer participatory learning so much as a competency currency. This amounts to hyperindividualization of the sought after skill set responding to a (mis)perceived competency employment marketplace.

Yet we should not be naïve about the costs or touted benefits. Universities are not principally service providers. They are knowledge producers. They develop and disseminate knowledge across a broad range of areas and constituencies, educating and informing a broad range of people professionally and for social and civic life more generally.

The impacts of uberization on the academy, and the humanities especially, are increasingly profound. Faculty, grown beleaguered, are accordingly less inclined to speak out either about the institutional challenges or the political climate more broadly. Indeed they are actively discouraged from engaging critically, and in any case have less time to do so. Faculty commitment to the institution has now become overwhelmingly to securing a livelihood rather than to an educational, intellectual, or political project. With a job like most other office work, faculty are likely to realize their driving intellectual interests extra-institutionally, in think tanks and working groups, political organizing and cultural production, collaborating with those sharing these interests, no matter their institutional location. Critical faculty, when not driven out or to silence, spend much of their critical efforts defending each other or the general right to express themselves or their vocal colleagues, unbounded by the narrowed institutional regulations. This of course reduces the time and energy they have to devote to critically address the pressing issues themselves.

The increasing scrutiny under which the academy generally and outspoken faculty especially tend to find themselves today has focused disproportionately acutely on the human sciences. This is not to say scientists have not drawn attention. Conservative politicians, for instance, have been especially vicious regarding the likes of Michael Mann for his seminal work on global warming, or Marc Edwards, the engineer who first brought to light the devastating lead contamination in the water supply of Flint, Michigan. But faculty in the human sciences tend more broadly to address issues of inequality, violence, discrimination, diversity, borders, cultural comprehension, and the like. In doing so they tend to take less conservative positions regarding those issues.

Generalized scrutiny operates at multiple scales: the microcosmic and invasively digital and the traditionally macroscopic. Microscopically, digital technology, as I suggested, enables tracking faculty and student interaction, work, and expression, all of which have footprints visible to contemporary technological audit. Macroscopically, the records generated through reviews, formal and informal student surveys, public profiles, and the like offer records more easily invoked today than in the past by critics wanting to curtail critical expression or activity. I am shorthanding all of this under the metaphor of "uberization," as it has taken its cue from the disposition and technological capacity to track, contain, and constrain that Uber-like platforms have made available and encouraged, while simultaneously claiming technoneutrality in terms of political commitment.

In any case, Uber-inspired service platforms across a broad range— restaurant, grocery, and package delivery, parking services, personal car rentals—are seeing increased operations costs, lower service provider wages, declining service quality, and bankruptcies.[7] Platform control hides behind the anonymous technological "neutrality" of algorithmically produced, crowdsourced data inputs, and judgment and recommendation outputs, none of which has reliable checks and balances. The immediate future is one of increasing robotification of skilling and smart algorithms autogenerating their own code. The pressures to downsize the human interface of learning, to delimit faculty determination of what and how things are valuable to be learned, of discounting *critical* knowledge and thinking capacity in every sense of the term will only intensify. As Uber's own administrative workforce (in contrast to its drivers) testifies, the impact will be to further narrow diversity, intellectually as much as demographically.[8] This is awfully narrow-cast, as corporations are increasingly shying away from university skillification training—corporations themselves are better at providing the technical skills they need on the particular job at hand—in favor of students capable of thinking, writing, listening, and working collaboratively.

Uber recently announced the intention to purchase $10 million worth of driverless cars. So it is joining the roboticizing of the workforce. In higher education we are increasingly facing the distinct possibility of a faceless future, teacherless courses, online everything. We should face this intensifying prospect of Uber U. with eyes wide open, counter-clickers firmly in hand.

Notes

1. The idea that the university is being "uberized" first occurred to me in conversation with Gregoire Chamayou at a workshop on the future of higher education organized by the University of California Humanities Research Institute, Goree Institute, Senegal, December 4–6, 2015. I am grateful also to Muriam Haleh Davis, Charles Heller, Caren Kaplan, Zen Marie, and Leigh-Ann Naidoo.
2. University of Michigan, "University of Michigan Funding."
3. American Academy of Arts and Sciences, "Public Research Universities."
4. Meranze and Newfield, "The $48 Fix."
5. Belkin and Korn, "Colleges' Use of Adjuncts."
6. Cook, "Life Is One Big Party."
7. Manjoo, "The Uber Model."
8. Ink 361, "@KendallBishop."

Works Cited

American Academy of Arts and Sciences. "Public Research Universities: Changes in State Funding." Lincoln Project: Excellence and Access in Public Higher Education, 2015. https://www.amacad.org/multimedia/pdfs/publications/research papersmonographs/PublicResearchUniv_ChangesInStateFunding.pdf.

Belkin, Douglas, and Melissa Korn. "Colleges' Use of Adjuncts Comes under Pressure." *Wall Street Journal,* February 16, 2015. http://www.wsj.com/articles /colleges-use-of-adjunct-instructors-comes-under-pressure-1424118108.

Cook, James. "Life Is One Big Party at 'Uberversity,' the Monthly Training Program in San Francisco That Uber Pays for New Employees to Attend." *Business Insider,* March 15, 2015. http://www.businessinsider.com/inside-uberversity -uber-staff-training-program-2015-3.

Ink 361. "@KendallBishop." Accessed February 7, 2017. http://ink361.com /app/users/ig-18950579/kendallbishop/photos/ig-906919036808925761_18950579.

Manjoo, Farhad. "The Uber Model, It Turns Out, Doesn't Translate." *New York Times,* March 23, 2016. http://www.nytimes.com/2016/03/24/technology/the -uber-model-it-turns-out-doesnt-translate.html?_r=0 23.

Meranze, Michael, and Christopher Newfield. "The $48 Fix: Reclaiming California's Master Plan for Higher Education." *Reclaim California Higher Education.* Accessed February 9, 2017. http://www.reclaimcahighered.org/48dollars.

University of Michigan. "University of Michigan Funding: A Snapshot." Accessed February 11, 2017. http://vpcomm.umich.edu/budget/fundingsnapshot/3.html.

Rationality, Racism, and Imagining Social Justice
David Palumbo-Liu

It is November 22, 2017. I have received useful comments and suggestions for revision from the editor of this volume and the press reader. Tomorrow is Thanksgiving and the university buildings are nearly deserted. I have carved out precisely this day to revise my draft; the sky is gray, my office is quiet, I sit down to write. Then I am reminded—on exactly this day, in 2014, Tamir Rice, a twelve-year-old black boy, was enjoying his preholiday in a public park in Cleveland, Ohio. It must have been cold then; the leaves had turned. Rice was not doing anything unusual; he was a young kid playing with a pellet gun. But guns in the hands of black people are automatically assumed to be lethal and aimed at people who need protection. Although the police dispatcher can be heard saying that the "weapon" is "probably fake" and the "perpetrator" "probably a juvenile," a police officer shot Tamir Rice to death.[1]

The prosecutor, Timothy J. McGinty, representing "the people," advised the Grand Jury not to press charges against the officer:

> Mr. McGinty said the fatal encounter had been a tragedy and a "perfect storm of human error, mistakes and miscommunications." But he said that enhancement of video from the scene had made it "indisputable" that Tamir, who was black, was drawing the pellet gun from his waistband when he was shot, either to hand it over to the officers or to show them that it was not a real firearm. He said that there was no reason for the officers to know that, and that the officer who fired, Timothy Loehmann, had a reason to fear for his life.[2]

In this essay, I urge us to linger, painfully, over the language employed here, for it is saturated with absolutes ("perfect," "indisputable," "no reason"). Somehow, despite the assurances of state language, two terrible and irretrievable things happened: Tamir Rice was killed, and the person who killed him was left unpunished. And this dyad of death and failure to find guilt is hardly without precedent (two years earlier another young black boy—Trayvon Martin, whose case I also discuss—was killed and his murderer exonerated) and hardly likely not to be repeated over and over again, as we have seen.

This is especially the case with the election of Donald Trump to the presidency, which has ushered in a dramatic increase in hate crimes, facilitated by the president himself, who has both refused to condemn in any serious manner the white supremacists and neo-Nazis who marched on the campus of the University of Virginia and were responsible for the death of the antifascist activist Heather Heyer, and who has been lavish in his condemnation of people like the NFL players who have "taken a knee" to draw attention to racial injustice; Trump infamously called those engaging in peaceful protest "sons of bitches."

The rise in expressions of antiblack, antibrown, anti-Muslim, anti-immigrant, antigay, and antitrans hatred is coterminous with cries of "reverse racism" and "white genocide," the supposed oppression of white males. These reversals of reality are encapsulated in the reaction to #BlackLivesMatter. Shortly after #BlackLivesMatter came into the view of the broad public, a defiant rebuttal shot forth: "All Lives Matter." There are a number of ways to read that. First, it could be seen as an expansive gesture meant to draw black lives into the larger global community, but a second, more accurate read would interpret it as a rebuttal and repudiation of #BlackLivesMatter, erasing the specificity of black lives under threat and under oppression. The move to universality appealed to a rational scheme as well as a sentimental one; the empathy lost in the process for the specific and very real grievances of blacks was accompanied by a rationalization that suggested that no special remedies would or should be forthcoming. A life is a life, period. In this essay, I suggest that a biologically driven, species-driven rationality—represented in the state's language surrounding the Tamir Rice killing—that disobliges itself from any serious address to history has to be met with a social challenge and a social sanction, if we are going to even start to approach social justice.

While the history of antiblack violence is centuries old, in the past few years this violence has come into public awareness by way of a number of cases that, perhaps thanks to social media, have achieved not only wide recognition but also wide public commentary. One case was that of the killing of Trayvon Martin. In 2012 I wrote in *Truthout*:

Since the acquittal of George Zimmerman Saturday for the death of Trayvon Martin, there have been thousands of tweets, dozens of blogs. Some are relieved by the verdict, others try to explain the legal basis. But most are part of a collective scream of outrage and grief. Of these latter, the predominant feeling is one of disbelief—how can the facts of the matter not bring some sort of punishment for Zimmerman? Any at all? How is he not guilty of taking the life of another human being who had done nothing to him of his own accord? As much as I get the legal reasoning—often delivered to us sanctimoniously and condescendingly by both legal scholars and those simply wanting to say the system *works*—we just don't understand how *fair* it is, how *rational* the decision was—my reaction to the verdict is very much that of Lawrence Bobo: "The most elemental facts of this case will never change. A teenager went out to buy Skittles and iced tea. At some point, he was confronted by a man with a gun who killed him. There is no universe I understand where this can be declared a noncriminal act. Not in a sane, just and racism-free universe."[3]

The decision of the grand jury not to indict Darren Wilson for the killing of Michael Brown Jr., the killers of Eric Garner, and the lack of justice in the deaths of Sandra Bland, Tanisha Anderson, Rekia Boyd, Shelly Frey, and other black men and women produces in many the same sense of disbelief and outrage. What we perhaps most react to is the complacency that we find in these cases, the acquiescence to a norm of violence and brutality—not only physical but also economic, political, and cultural. This normalcy, this business as usual, is underwritten not only by entrenched sentiments, it is also aided and abetted by a seemingly neutral, objective, and inescapable rationality. When Lawrence Bobo speaks of his sense of disbelief, appealing to the notion of a "sane, . . . racism-free" universe, we need to query our assumptions about the coexistence of such terms. I want to focus specifically on the ideas of reasonableness and rationality, as delivered in language, and how they may not align with the absence of racism but sometimes, if not often, enable it. My argument is that sometimes language leads us astray, obscures a clear vision to truth and justice, and that sometimes it simply fails us—it fails to capture the human significance of injustice and fails to form lines of solidarity.

At any moment we are confronted with calls for solidarity; think of the horrific and illegal Israeli attack on Gaza, a continuation of the dispossession and delegitimization of the Palestinian people in both the Occupied Palestinian Territories and the state of Israel, which has resulted in one of the most powerful and urgent calls for solidarity emanating from Palestinian civil society: the Boycott, Divestment, and Sanctions movement. But think too of the need always to reflect back on what we are signing on to, as with the swelling of sympathy worldwide after the Charlie Hebdo killings and the hashtag #JeSuisCharlie. I will return to that latter case at the end of my essay. The point I want to stress here is that calls for both individual and collective acts of solidarity need to carefully attend to the ways history is delivered to us in language that is anything but neutral, and that struggles over language and who gets to say what, and who is found credible, are the most important struggles we can engage in.

It is in struggling to find forms of adequate ethical response and action that the humanities can help us imagine social justice, above and beyond what is available to us now. Some of the most urgent questions before us in this regard are the following: How can the humanities help us articulate something that seems intuitively wrong but might be exactly what we need under these conditions of brutal rationality, deadly normalcy, and dulled, stultified thinking—that is, an irrational, abnormal, even perverse imagining of something other than what we have? How can we use the imagination precisely to instantiate mechanisms that deliver justice in more adequate ways? Another way of saying all this: How can we imagine a politically effective negative dialectic that pushes back against the stultifying language of rationalized oppression?

I would suggest that one way to think of this is to consider the nature of hate crime legislation. Hate crimes need to be seen as having a social life (as opposed to a merely political or legal existence). They are an added marker of social abhorrence, over and beyond the penalty for a predicate offense. Generally, prosecution under a hate crime statute requires that the individual committed some predicate offense set out in the statute with the animus specified in a hate crime statute, with the statute operating to enhance the punishment imposed for the predicate offense. The fact that a hate crime is one that marks an additional penalty on top of a predicate crime reveals the extra sanction society places on the crime—first recognizing and then factoring in "hate"—shows the margin of the social sanction over and above the condemnation of the predicate offense. Hate crime prosecution not only recognizes an added wrong but also signals to the victims of hate crimes society's acknowledgment of their particular vulnerability—in other words, society's recognition that black lives matter, expressed in law. Hate crimes are essential supplements that update our social sanctions, recognizing the evolution of hatred. And yet, not unexpectedly, hate crimes are difficult to prosecute, given our rationalization of racism. Thus what we see in hate crimes is the vacillation between intimations of and aspirations toward justice, and the residual and still strong reluctance to see racial hatred as a special category.

This notion that alongside or beyond legal punishment there can be an extra marker of blame or abhorrence emanating from the social world that may or may not find any recourse in existing law is found in Hannah Arendt's comments on the prosecution of war criminals. Of course, the analogy is not exact, but I want to focus on this idea of social abhorrence over and beyond what can be neatly contained within the law and its judgment. Arendt first raises "the question of *legal* punishment, punishment that is usually justified on one of the following grounds: the need of society to be protected against crime, the improvement of the criminal, the deterring force of the warning example for potential criminals, and, finally, retributive justice." She then says, "A moment of reflection will convince you that none of these grounds is valid for the punishment of the so-called war criminals: these people were not ordinary criminals and hardly any one of them can reasonably be expected to commit further crimes; society is in no need of being protected from them." Arendt then goes on to show that none of the other reasons pertains to war criminals, concluding, "Here we are, demanding and meting a punishment in accordance with our sense of justice, while, on the other hand, the same sense of justice informs us that all our previous notions about punishment and justification have failed us."[4]

In a similar manner, given the current rise of white supremacy and fascism, we must not let not only hate speech but also, and more important, the violence that that hate speech feeds on and enables, be relegated to simply a matter of "free speech" and managed by that liberal accommodation. As Meleiza Figueroa and I wrote in a piece about the antifascist protests at Berkeley:

> Right-wing speaking events—including the "Free Speech Week" scheduled for late September at Berkeley, featuring the odious trifecta of Yiannopoulos, Coulter, and Steve Bannon—are part of an

increasingly coordinated nationwide effort among far-right groups to recruit on college campuses. Using free speech as a wedge to silence dissent and discredit opposition, they intend to radicalize white youth by waging psychological warfare on academic leftists, social-justice organizations, and minorities. It should be no surprise that Jeremy Christian, white-supremacist murderer of two men in Portland, cried out "Free speech or die!" during his day in court. For white supremacists, the push for free speech is directly connected to their campaigns of terror.[5]

This is at the crux of the matter: How can a society voice a grievance *over and above* what is considered rationally proper, civil, operative, functional? How can we voice extraordinary outrage over injustice in ways that are socially and politically meaningful and useful? How can what passes as rational or reasonable be decentered and another way of thinking instantiated, or at least imagined and shared? To do this, I want to have us consider the relationship between rationality, language, and justice, and how they operate in times of crisis, again, specifically when the world seems upside down.

Let's return to that quotation from Bobo, his evocation of a "sane, just and racism-free universe."[6] What he was doing there was, of course, marking the distance between a world most of us aspire to and would want to help bring about, and the world as we know it, which is decidedly insane, unjust, and full of racism. But even as we note that, we must acknowledge that for far too many people, the world is precisely sane and just. That's the problem. How can some people continue to think, as they and generations have for decades, that things are just fine, that the world in fact works the way it ought to?

Or, let me amend that—it's not exactly fine, because we have crime, poverty, disease, illiteracy, et cetera. And we have people on both the liberal and conservative sides drawing our attention to these issues. Some liberals say that there is something structural in all this, that structural racism goes far back into our history and that the role of the liberal state is to make adjustments to lessen the burden and increase opportunity. Conservatives, on the other hand, are happy to blame minorities themselves for some essential lack or pathology that no matter of state intervention can help. My answer to those rationalizations is to focus our eyes and our imaginative capacities elsewhere. We have to imagine the historical circumstances that, while they benefited some, turned the worlds of others entirely upside down, in the waves of enslavement, dispossession, and death, that can be attributed not to some defect in their constitution but rather to the raw exercise of power over others, an exercise of power that seeks legitimacy and even an imperative to act so by means of rationality.

Frantz Fanon speaks clearly of the racialization of reason in *Black Skins, White Masks*:

> The psychoanalysts say that nothing is more traumatizing for the young child than his encounters with what is rational. I would personally say that for a man whose only weapon is reason there is nothing more neurotic than contact with unreason.
>
> I felt knife blades open within me. I resolved to defend myself. As a good tactician, I intended to rationalize the world and show the white man he was mistaken. . . . With enthusiasm I set to cataloguing and probing my surroundings. As times changed, one had seen the Catholic religion at first justify and then condemn slavery and prejudices. But by referring everything to the idea of the dignity of man, one had ripped prejudice to shreds. After much reluctance, the scientists had conceded that the Negro was a human being; in vivo and in vitro the Negro had proved analogous to the white man: the same morphology, the same histology. Reason was confident on every level. I put all the parts back together. But I had to change my tune.
>
> That victory played cat and mouse; it made a fool of me. As the other put it, when I was present, it was not; when it was there, I was no longer. In the abstract there was agreement: the Negro is a human being. That is to say, amended the less firmly convinced, that like us he has a heart on the left side.[7]

The trajectory of this passage is clear: Fanon, a man of reason, is confounded by the irrational racism of the white man and confidently confronts it armed, precisely, with reason. He "catalogues his world" in an effort to trace and discover the legacies of racism and irrationality and yet finds that those forms have morphed and changed into various guises in the course of history, the final one being of accommodation— the Negro is found to be, after all, human. And yet that humanity was qualified and liable to be withdrawn. Here Fanon speaks of the absolute confinement of race in terms of sexuality, but that is just the most extreme case. The point is that the designation of humanness is always open to negotiation, and for the black man, it is to be always negotiated from a position of weakness. Ultimately Fanon admits defeat, for the moment:

> I had rationalized the world and the world had rejected me on the basis of color prejudice. Since no agreement was possible on the level of reason, I threw myself back toward unreason. It was up to the white man to be more irrational than I. Out of the necessities of my struggle I had chosen the method of regression, but the fact remained that it was an unfamiliar weapon; here I am at home; I am made of the irrational; I wade in the irrational.[8]

Here, and throughout, I will be speaking about rationality in a particular manner; I want to use it along with notions of normalcy and civility. Why do that? Because rationality is often evoked to make a claim for a norm; norms are justified by being the end product of a process of social reasoning, and it is considered at once irrational and uncivil to weigh in against norms. In terms of the humanities, such norms are tested out and critiqued. It is precisely the humanities that give us a working vocabulary with which to address these issues. It is up to us to make novel, imaginative, and sometimes audacious use of the tools.

Let me now bring together the two strands of my essay; both are entwined around the notion of a world turned upside down. We in the humanities pay particular attention to language; it is the essential core of literary studies. As such, it is a precise indicator when things go bad, or worse. And worse, in my opinion, is when injustice and violence become acceptable and normal, albeit lamented, facts of the world. They become rationalized, excused, and complaints against them are derided as irrational, or, in another articulation, naïve, idealistic, unrealistic. I am arguing that the humanities, properly attuned to the complexity of language and the importance of thinking in a deep historical manner, are our indispensable aids in working together in solidarity—not in blind and thoughtless solidarity, but in more sustainable and just solidarity, to help put a more just world in place. The humanities can help us judge how language can both obfuscate and clarify, depending largely on questions of history and power. It can turn things right side up but also invert things, and, confoundingly, as it does so it can claim to do the opposite. Literature requires vigilance and attention.

It is precisely in times of crisis that language is most needed, and yet it is also in times of crisis that it is most vulnerable, and sometimes even depleted. It is no accident that the great Nigerian author Chinua Achebe would evoke the notion of the world being upside down via a linguistic act. This phrase takes place in his novel *No Longer at Ease*. The events take place as the protagonist, Obi, returns to his village after his education in England:

> Obi knew the refrain, he tried to translate it into English, and for the first time its real meaning dawned on him. . . .
>
> On the face of it there was no kind of logic or meaning in the song. But as Obi turned it round and round in his mind, he was struck by the wealth of association that even such a mediocre song could have. First of all it was unheard of for a man to seize his in-law and kill him. To the Ibo mind it was the height of treachery. Did not the elders say that a man's in-law was his *ch'i*, his personal god? Set against this was another great betrayal; a paddle that begins suddenly to talk in a language which its master, the fisherman, does not understand. In short, then, thought Obi. The burden of the song was "the world turned upside down." He was pleased with his exegesis and began to search in his mind for other songs that could be given the same treatment. But the song of the traders was now so loud and spicy that he could not concentrate on this thinking.[9]

What exactly has happened here? Well, a lot—the possibilities of language (between even a paddle and a fisherman), ethics, music, culture, knowledge. But let me concentrate on just a few things. First of all, this is a song Obi "knows." That is, he has some preexisting sense of what it means. But his very attempt to translate it, to bring that cultural knowledge into another cultural form, yields something completely different. Because of his new knowledge of English, he is now set apart from the traders—he comes to know their song but in a different language. In short, he himself is a walking, talking example of the new, uneasy world of the colonial subject. And the current violence in Nigeria must be placed in the lineage of such acts of barbarism. In this context, we should look back to Fanon and the complex contradictions of language and reason he found himself enmeshed in. As a political logician, Fanon takes on rationality in its instrumentalized form; as a writer of fiction, Achebe takes up the precarious history of the transition from African orality to colonial narrativity. In both cases we see the struggle to make visible a rupture, a contradiction, an epistemological distance where the language of power has glossed over all those things and naturalized them. The humanities has to precisely denaturalize such language and make its functioning anything but inevitable.

In one of the greatest works of modern oratory, Toni Morrison includes this statement in her Nobel Prize acceptance speech:

> The systematic looting of language can be recognized by the tendency of its users to forgo its nuanced, complex, mid-wifery properties for menace and subjugation. Oppressive language does more than represent violence; it is violence; does more than represent the limits of knowledge; it limits knowledge. Whether it is obscuring state language or the faux-language of mindless media; whether it is the proud but calcified language of the academy or the commodity driven language of science; whether it is the malign language of law-without-ethics, or language designed for the estrangement of minorities, hiding its racist plunder in its literary cheek—it must be rejected, altered and exposed. It is the language that drinks blood, laps vulnerabilities, tucks its fascist boots under crinolines of respectability and patriotism as it moves relentlessly toward the bottom line and the bottomed-out mind. Sexist language, racist language, theistic language—all are typical of the policing languages of mastery, and cannot, do not permit new knowledge or encourage the mutual exchange of ideas.[10]

Under the conditions that pervert language and turn it upside down, norms are trotted out to precisely ensure that the status quo continues unimpeached.

For sustained work for social justice to occur, we must carve out space for both rationality and irrationality, civility and unruliness. The instantiation and imposition of rationality and civility cannot be top-down, imposed, or oppressive. It must be freely given in order to address the crisis. Norms, rationality, and civility are not dispensable. But they are tools that we must use wisely and self-consciously, as they both endow rights and deny rights too.

If the language of assent has to be arrived at mutually, so do the attributions of rationality and reason. I am not so idealistic as to believe that we can ever reach a perfect consensus on either; again, the key for me is for us to understand the nature of our compromises and commitments.

Let me end by sharing my thoughts with you on the Charlie Hebdo killings, or, rather, on the spontaneous demonstrations that sprang up immediately after, and use this event to bring us back to some of the concerns I raised at the beginning of this essay about #AllLivesMatter. Again we find language being a powerful consolidating force. But as I argue here, that consolidation should not automatically be seen as entirely positive. For many, but not all commentators, this terrible event could be broken down into a clash of civilizations, between the enlightened West and the irrational East. This was not the most immediate reading for many who participated in the JeSuisCharlie demonstrations, but this was the subtitle I had in mind as I witnessed the events that unfolded. I would like to conclude by reflecting on those events, specifically as they are linked to rationality, racism, and justice.

The horrific summary execution of a dozen members of the editorial staff of the French satiric magazine *Charlie Hebdo* has drawn nearly global outrage and grief. Commentators have been quick to file op-eds, and I am no different. However, rather than trying to speak on the issues of race, religion, fundamentalism, terrorism, free speech, or French society and politics, I want to focus on the tidal wave of demonstrations and social media campaigns that unabashedly and passionately declare an apparently seamless bond of identification. "#ICan'tBreathe" is now joined by "#JeSuisCharlie."

The aerial photos over New York City, and now over Paris, showing the multitudes of grieving, angry people is for me both impressive and frightening. Emotion is always more powerful than reason. Now, certainly if you asked any one of the demonstrators at these events what were their reasons for being there and for declaring their identification with Eric Garner or *Charlie Hebdo*, you would very quickly get a barrage of ready responses. But they would likely be telegraphic, formulaic. They would both benefit and suffer from the power of immediacy.

Now such pronouncements of identification have always been around. The most memorable of the postwar era was probably John F. Kennedy's "Ich bin ein Berliner" (I am a Berliner) speech in 1963, on the steps of Rathaus Schöneberg; they are a standard part of our rhetorical repertoire. I neither endorse nor condemn #ICan'tBreathe or #JeSuisCharlie, but I urge us to pause and consider just in how many ways these acts of

identification can function. Here are three—they are, by no means, mutually exclusive or clearly demarcated; none of them is *necessarily* good or
bad. They are the following: empathy, solidarity, and identification.

Empathy comes up when we can imagine the suffering, fear, and pain
of others. As the eighteenth-century political and economic theorist Adam
Smith notes in his *Theory of Moral Sentiments*, one of the fundamentals
of social life is the ability to imagine ourselves in a similar situation as
others; that is how people are bound together. This is a rich and good
capacity in human beings. But as much as I appreciate it, I also question
to whom we extend our empathy. This specifies, and narrows, our cele-
bration of empathy. We can certainly not attend to all the world's worthy
subjects of empathy, but we are morally responsible for accounting for
whom we empathize with, and those whose pain, death, and suffering
we ignore, even if their suffering is just as bad, or even worse, than the
ones we care for. Why don't people (especially in the "developed" countries) fill our streets and plazas when we learn of the deaths of those
killed—just as brutally and emphatically—in Africa, Asia, Latin America?
By either automatic rifle fire or what Rob Nixon calls the "slow violence"
of economic, political, environmental, cultural strangulation? What circumscribes our outrage, and our willingness to act? If it turns out that we
empathize with people who are mostly like us, then that is a pretty limited form of empathy—resembling more self-love. Empathy, in this case,
solidifies long-standing biases, and this is what I fear might well be hap-
pening to some degree in the case of the #JeSuisCharlie demonstrations.

Solidarity means signing on to whatever cause seems to be presented by
those who have suffered. This is a more engaged form of protest, because
it does not stop at mere pity and empathy—it promises future action. But
what actions are sanctioned and legitimized by one's identification with
the victims of violence? There are already iconic signs attesting to solidarity with *Charlie Hebdo*, but what, exactly, are we now agreeing to do, in
"solidarity"? The simplest and most compelling "cause" *Charlie Hebdo*
now stands for in the eyes of most is a free press and free speech. But
are we not forgetting what this publication "satirized," and how? *Charlie Hebdo* had previously been the center of controversy, death threats,
and fire-bombing in 2011 over its special issue entitled "Charia Hebdo,"
which featured a cartoon depicting the Islamic prophet Mohammed as
its editor in chief. Now, those in the West might shrug this off as edgy
satire, but to not imagine that those whose religion was being parodied

came from a different cultural background than those who produced the image, and to assert that those who might be offended should nonetheless read the satire as if they were not from an Islamic background, bespeaks arrogance. If we are absolute in defending the depiction of anything, in any way, we had better be prepared to be on the streets for any horrific, offensive, immoral, pornographic image that might be presented to us. Or else, as I said before, be held accountable for the particularity of our "solidarity."

Finally, and most problematic for me, is the notion of identification. #ICan'tBreathe is a powerful symbol of solidarity and, like all symbols, a bit false. Some of us can and will always be able to breathe just fine. Again, the idea is not to give up on solidarity; it is rather to respect and defer to the real differences that injustice produces, understanding who the real and likely victims are, and acting with that knowledge and humility. And here is where the two cases are distinct, for they tap into two different kinds of grievances.

#ICan'tBreathe gathered enormous support because we in the United States have seen the murder of black and brown men (and women and children) take place over and over again throughout our history, and seen their killers escape justice in nearly all these cases. The killing of Eric Garner, captured on video—the relentless, illegal, and unnecessary strangulation of a human being, followed by the exoneration of his killer—tapped into a long history of such violence. We had had enough. Those marching are victims or likely victims of such violence, and others who understand the structural racism that undergirds these acts and the near impunity with which such killers perform such acts. What is required nonetheless, if such antiracist movements are to be successful, is a calibrated understanding of the actual historical realities of racism in the United States.

The case of JeSuisCharlieHebdo is somewhat different, but it demands the same self-reflection and inspection of the historical record. The situation of Arabs and those of the Islamic faith in France has been one of long-standing oppression and racism, dating back to France's colonial projects. Like all colonizers, French racists have legitimized their oppression of and hatred for Arabs and others by denigrating their culture and beliefs and holding the values of the Western liberalism tradition as the only ones worth maintaining. What we in the U.S. call "multiculturalism" simply does not exist in France. There the keyword is "integration," which means, again, the "submission" of others to the French model—hence the satiric irony of the title of the Houellebecq novel. And since the terrorist attacks of 9/11, what Samuel Huntington called the "clash of civilizations" rhetoric has been exploited to further legitimize the notion that some peoples just cannot be "integrated." What many see in the terrible killings of the staff of *Charlie Hebdo* is, in fact, a confirmation of that belief: "these people" are not really people at all; despite their perfect, accentless French, they have no respect for free speech; they are irremediable terrorists at heart. I think we need to watch out for that, while not giving up our grieving and outrage at the killings.

So what does it really mean to say "I am Charlie Hebdo"? This can run the gamut of "I am a defender of free speech" (see above) to "I think Islam is ridiculous and dangerous" to "I am a rabid French chauvinist." Let me be clear—I am not saying that *Charlie Hebdo* was necessarily representing any of those notions, at least not in the way any of us might interpret those characterizations; I am saying that people who are all these things and more can rally together, all leaning on each other without knowing what new strange bedfellows they (or we) have joined. Not unlike the proliferation of yellow ribbons that popped up after 9/11, when it soon became clear that that sign of empathy, solidarity, identification meant everything from pity for the victims of the attack to a willingness to visit nuclear weapons upon whoever we felt was responsible, to a carte blanche for the United States to do anything it pleased on the world stage. Frankly, when I saw the photographs of demonstrators in France, taken from on high, the people's faces invisible, my worst fear was that so much of that energy would be translated into adding fuel to long-standing anti-Islam hatred, for lack of any better channel for all that anger, fear, shock, and awe.

This terrible event took place in a situation already inflamed with racial and religious, even "civilizational" tensions, not to mention political ones. Where will all this empathy, solidarity, and identification flow? It is impossible to predict because these events take place within a complex set of preexisting conditions. One would hope that these demonstrations in France will not fuel precisely the kinds of extreme and intolerant and instrumentalized hatred and violence that we found in the murderers. The best way to identify with *Charlie Hebdo* would be to not give in to that mode of identification and not to see others as caricatures, stereotypes, or cardboard figures. If we end up taking on that aspect of *Charlie Hebdo*, in whatever small or big way, we would have made a very bad choice of identity.

Let me end by saying that some worlds need to be turned upside down. As I said at the very beginning, this is a necessary act of negative dialectics—negating the negation. Sometimes norms that we have become habituated to need to be broken; what passes for reason, rationality, civility, needs to be uprooted. Here is how James Baldwin writes on the subject, as he addresses his nephew on the hundredth anniversary of Emancipation:

> To act is to be committed, and to be committed is to be in danger. In this case, the danger, in the minds of most white Americans, is the loss of their identity. Try to imagine how you would feel if you woke up one morning to find the sun shining and all the stars aflame. You would be frightened because it is out of the order of nature. Any upheaval in the universe is terrifying because it so profoundly attacks one's sense of one's own reality. Well, the black man has functioned in the white man's world as a fixed star, as an immovable pillar; and as he moves out of his place, heaven and earth are shaken to their foundations.[11]

Our task of course is to imagine, and work to realize, a new foundation that is just, righteous, and humane for all.

Notes

1. "Tamir Rice Shooting Video."
2. Williams and Smith, "Cleveland Officer."
3. Palumbo-Liu, "On the Zimmerman Verdict."
4. Arendt, "Personal Responsibility," 25, 26.
5. Figueroa and Palumbo-Liu, "Why Berkeley's Battle."
6. Bobo, "Trayvon Martin."
7. Fanon, *Black Skin, White Masks*, 118.
8. Ibid.,123.
9. Achebe, *No Longer at Ease*, 53.
10. Morrison, "Nobel Lecture."
11. Baldwin, *The Fire Next Time*, 9.

Works Cited

Achebe, Chinua. *No Longer at Ease*. New York: Anchor Doubleday, 1960.
Arendt, Hannah. "Personal Responsibility under Dictatorship." In Arendt, *Responsibility and Judgment*. New York: Schocken, 2003.

Baldwin, James. *The Fire Next Time*. New York: Vintage Press, 1993.

Bobo, Lawrence D. "Trayvon Martin: Florida Jury's Not Guilty Verdict 'Failed Us.'" *Bay State Banner* (Dorchester, Mass.), July 17, 2013. http://baystatebanner .com/news/2013/jul/17/trayvon-martin-florida-jurys-not-guilty-verdict-fa/ ?page=1.

Fanon Frantz. *Black Skin, White Masks*. New York: Grove Weidenfeld, 1967.

Figueroa, Meleiza, and David Palumbo-Liu. "Why Berkeley's Battle against White Supremacy Is Not about Free Speech." *The Nation*, September 8, 2017. https:// www.thenation.com/article/why-berkeleys-battle-against-white-supremacy-is -not-about-free-speech/.

Jordan, June. "Civil Wars." In *Civil Wars*. New York: Simon and Schuster, 1981.

Lockwood, Preston. "Henry James's First Interview." *New York Times*, March 21, 1915. http://query.nytimes.com/gst/abstract.html?res=9F06E3D61439EF3 2A25752C2A9659C946496D6CF&legacy=true.

Morrison, Toni. "Nobel Lecture." December 7, 1993. https://www.nobelprize.org /nobel_prizes/literature/laureates/1993/morrison-lecture.html.

Palumbo-Liu, David. "On the Zimmerman Verdict: Sympathy for the Devil." *Truthout,* July 16, 2013. http://www.truth-out.org/speakout/item/17599-on -the-zimmerman-verdict-sympathy-for-the-devil.

———. "The Problem with #JeSuisCharlie: That Kind of Solidarity Comes with Baggage." *Salon*, January11, 2015. https://www.salon.com/2015/01 /11/the_problem_with_je_suis_charlie_that_kind_of_solidarity_comes_with _baggage/.

"Tamir Rice Shooting Video: Footage Shows Cleveland Cops Shoot Boy 2 Seconds after Arriving." YouTube, November 26, 2014. https://www.youtube.com /watch?v=mSCftESyKyU&feature=youtu.be/.

Williams, Timothy, and Mitch Smith. "Cleveland Officer Will Not Face Charges in Tamir Rice Shooting Death." *New York Times*, December 28, 2015. https:// www.nytimes.com/2015/12/29/us/tamir-rice-police-shootiing-cleveland.html.

Rage and Beauty: Celebrating Complexity, Democracy, and the Humanities

Robert D. Newman

One of the most fascinating things I have found in my recent return to the Carolinas, where I did my graduate work three decades ago, after having spent the past fourteen years in Salt Lake City, Utah, where the prevailing subtext in many conversations as well as policy issues and political debates centered around the Mormon/non-Mormon divide, is how, even during the tenure of our first African American president, the prevailing subtext still centers on race. Granted, it is an issue that pervades much of the country, but many of the seeds of the issue remain grounded in the South, although often nuanced in rhetoric and covert policy and practice. As we talk about the country's shifts in so many directions, exploring honestly and in depth the reasons behind divides and then engaging in civil discourse and study to bridge them remain the crucial challenges and the primary obstacles toward our true progress as a democratic and civil society. Interrogating and bridging are the core methodologies in humanities research and teaching; thus, I would argue, a humanities perspective is essential to our understanding and our success personally and collectively as citizens, to the success of our mission as educators and scholars, and to our ability to address the intractable problems—from climate change to immigration to national security to inequality to the proper exercise of critical judgment—that face us and require pluralistic analysis, recommendations, and implementation in order to be overcome.

Before discussing the challenges to the humanities and how we might better address those challenges, I would like to offer a story that helps illustrate the complexities of interrogation and bridging. It's an old story about the pope and the chief rabbi of Italy:

> Several centuries ago, the pope decreed that all the Jews had to leave
> Italy. There was, of course, a huge outcry from the Jewish community,

so the pope offered a deal. He would have a religious debate with a
leader of the Jewish community. If the Jewish leader won the debate,
the Jews would be permitted to stay in Italy. If the pope won, the Jews
would have to leave.

The Jewish community met and picked an aged rabbi, Moishe,
to represent them in the debate. Rabbi Moishe, however, could not
speak Latin and the pope could not speak Yiddish, so it was decided
it would be a silent debate.

On the day of the great debate the pope and Rabbi Moishe sat
opposite each other for a full minute before the pope raised his hand
and showed three fingers. Rabbi Moishe looked back and raised one
finger.

Next, the pope waved his finger around his head. Rabbi Moishe
pointed to the ground where he sat. The pope then brought out a
communion wafer and a chalice of wine. Rabbi Moishe pulled out an
apple. With that, the pope stood up and said, "I concede the debate.
This man has bested me. The Jews can stay."

Later, the cardinals gathered around the pope, asking him what
had happened. The pope said, "First I held up three fingers to represent the Trinity. He responded by holding up one finger to remind
me that there was still one God common to both our religions. Then
I waved my finger around me to show him that God was all around
us. He responded by pointing to the ground to show that God was
also right here with us. I pulled out the wine and the wafer to show
that God absolves us of our sins. He pulled out an apple to remind
me of original sin. He had an answer for everything. What could
I do?"

Meanwhile, the Jewish community crowded around Rabbi
Moishe, asking what happened. "Well," said Moishe, "first he said
to me, 'You Jews have three days to get out of here.' So I said to him,
'Not one of us is going to leave.' Then he tells me the whole city
would be cleared of Jews. So I said to him, 'Listen here, Mr. Pope, the
Jews . . . we stay right here!' "

"And then?" asked a woman.

"Who knows?" said Rabbi Moishe. "We broke for lunch."

Now our political and religious debates are seldom silent and are
typically perpetuated rather than solved through misunderstanding. And

although it may seem remote, steeped as we have been in a presidential campaign premised on meandering sensationalism and unsubstantiated assertions, we look to authenticity, to enduring truths to help us salvage reason and sense in the jumble of mixed messages we receive steadily. When I listen to some of the recent political declarations, I am reminded of the great Hollywood producer Samuel Goldwyn, who offered this advice to aspiring actresses: "The most important thing about acting is sincerity. If you can fake that, you've got it made."

The mission of the humanities is to expose rather than create shams, to root out the sources of and to rectify bogus claims and unsubstantiated assertions. We are all about storytelling, but as a revelation of truth and understanding, not for reckless self-promotion.

These core methodologies—interrogating and bridging—are mutually connected. To bridge one must first interrogate. But interrogation does not permit us to dwell in comfort zones and is born from a healthy skepticism, as distinct from cynicism, that often makes humanists irritating to themselves and others in their perpetual dissatisfaction with the norm. A certain unease within the active mind is fundamental to the human condition. Despite all the self-help manuals, we simply cannot leave well enough alone.

Many of the difficulties associated with the humanities rest in those tireless probings, nuances, and unsettlings. Critical thinking and intelligent questioning are not the stuff of inertia and ease, and the status quo does not benefit from them. The systematic attempts to marginalize the humanities seen in political rhetoric, marketing misinformation and its consumption by parents and students, and in the priorities sometimes established by some university administrators, underscore a neoliberal agenda that couches everything in terms of short-term profit and commodification of natural and human attributes. "Life, liberty and the pursuit of happiness" in this dystopian scenario becomes "Profit, profit, and the pursuit of profit." "We the people" becomes "We the economically elite," and the message has been channeled through stereotyping, divisiveness, and fearmongering that seethes with rage and dupes those who are maligned into a false sense of power in maligning others.

Making fun of the humanities as esoteric and impractical is nothing new; humanists themselves have indulged in this playful poking at least as much as nonhumanists. Aristophanes ridicules metaphysical conundrums in *The Clouds* when he depicts Socrates asking such questions as whether a gnat buzzes through its nose or its anus, a ludicrous early version of contemplating how many angels fit on the head of a pin.

But unlike the sciences, much of our appeal is grounded in our allegiance to mystery and the miraculous, a fidelity to the ungraspable, to the riddle that dwells in the heart of metaphor, and to empathy. Keats labeled our poetic capacity to reach into the spirit of someone or something distinct from ourselves "negative capability." William Empson called ambiguity the core quality of poetic beauty. Furthermore, the humanities, unlike the sciences, are premised on studying thoughts that now are scientifically untenable or artistic and literary styles that have become archaic. As Stephen Greenblatt has stated, humanists "begin with the desire to speak with the dead."[1] Such an attachment to the intangible and historical renders us easy targets for charges of irrelevance.

The culture wars of the 1990s challenged traditional disciplinary lenses and foregrounded previously marginalized political currents that threw the profession into a quandary with which it still struggles over relevance, subject matter, and methodology. The debates over whether or not race, class, gender, and sexuality should supplant aesthetic devices for unlocking the secrets stored within texts forced humanists to confront their traditional identities. But the debates centered on how we should approach the humanities, not, as they now do, over whether or not the humanities should continue to be funded as a legitimate field of study. The emergence of the latter debate has created a dire and destabilizing state of affairs from which we are increasingly reeling.

Contemporary humanities education has become multifaceted in its complications, a feature of its continuous unfolding, but also a challenge to its sustainability. The headlong rush of state legislatures and both public and private universities into support of STEM programs at the expense of, rather than as complementary to, humanities programs masks the fact that majors in both the physical sciences and mathematics have diminished more rapidly than those in the humanities, that half of those who graduate in STEM fields are not working in those fields after ten years but do not possess the foundational skills necessary for adaptability in a changing workforce that are taught in the humanities. But many institutions of higher learning have seized this one-dimensional trajectory, the logical outcome of which is that they become little more than vo-tech schools with football teams. We in the humanities still are committed to breadth of learning and a respect for the pursuit of knowledge for knowledge's sake, akin to the frontier spirit that propelled us as a nation, the consecration of discovery as a foundational and sacred principle of who we are and why we are here.

While it is easy to suggest that the study of the humanities is elitist given the need to secure good paying jobs that result from direct vocational training, what can be more elitist than arguing that learning about literature, history, philosophy, foreign cultures, and languages should be strictly the purview of the wealthy who do not have to concern themselves with job training?

Although some argue the humanities cannot cure cancer, cannot win a war against terrorists, and cannot increase your paycheck and therefore should take a backseat to those enterprises that can, consider the following: Without the ability to listen carefully to and engage with a patient's narrative, in other words to take a good case history, early detection and prevention of many cancers do not occur. And for those who must endure cancer treatment or make critical decisions regarding how they live and sometimes how they die, humanities touchstones matter as much as chemical interventions. As for the war on terror, perhaps an in-depth study of history by the occupants of the White House in 2003 might have prevented us from fighting ISIS today. Kenneth Burke wrote of literature as providing "equipment for living."[2] Indeed humanities skills offer a multifaceted and adaptable toolbox for navigating career shifts and changing workforce demands. And it is a statistical fact that liberal arts majors earn more during their lifetimes than business majors.

The humanities are as central to learning and to life as they always have been, but their tangible outcomes are more difficult to measure than other disciplines. The production and dissemination of knowledge cannot be counted like the number of widgets on an assembly line. How do we measure how a thesis formulated in an essay on literature finds its way into discussions about how we approach historical events that, over the course of several years, dynamically change the discipline or transform how teachers construct a syllabus? Yet articles about nineteenth-century slave narratives and women's domestic journals did just that. Or how a passage gleaned from one publication influences a classroom presentation by another professor who has read it, that in turn catches the imagination of an undergraduate student who goes on to apply it to her own invention or to a repurposing of her life.

The practice of humanities scholarship traditionally has been viewed as a monastic enterprise, a retreat from the daily trials and tribulations of worldly affairs in order to concentrate intellectually. However, much of the argument for preserving the study and teaching of humanities relies on its connections to the foundations of democratic thinking. From Socrates onward, the ability to reason rigorously and flexibly has been thought to undergird democracy. Indeed Jonathan Arac has argued that, without the democratic claim, humanists would have "nothing important to do."[3]

Martha Nussbaum has argued for universal norms to improve justice for women globally, refuting cultural relativism, especially regarding practices such as genital mutilation, as an approach that offers the "sort of moral collapse depicted by Dante when he describes the crowd of souls who mill around the vestibule of hell, dragging their banner now one way now another, never willing to set it down and take a definite stand on any moral or political question. Such people, he implies, are the most despicable of all. They can't even get into hell because they have not been willing to stand for anything in life."[4] We need to stand for what we always have stood for—the understanding and elevation of the human condition—and we need to use our rhetorical skills to make sure the public understands this and recognizes it as an essential need.

In an op-ed in the *New York Times*, "Will the Humanities Save Us?," Stanley Fish wrote:

> Do the humanities ennoble? And for that matter, is it the business of the humanities, or of any other area of academic study, to save us? The answer in both cases, I think, is no. The premise of secular humanism (or of just old-fashioned humanism) is that the examples of action and thought portrayed in the enduring works of literature, philosophy and history can create in readers the desire to emulate them. . . .
>
> It's a pretty idea, but there is no evidence to support it and a lot of evidence against it. If it were true, the most generous, patient, good-hearted and honest people on earth would be the members of literature and philosophy departments, who spend every waking hour with great books and great thoughts, and as someone who's been there (for 45 years) I can tell you it just isn't so. Teachers and students of literature and philosophy don't learn how to be good and wise; they learn how to analyze literary effects and to distinguish between

different accounts of the foundations of knowledge. . . . Teachers of literature and philosophy are competent in a subject, not in a ministry. It is not the business of the humanities to save us, no more than it is their business to bring revenue to a state or a university.[5]

Let us bracket the concluding comment about the business of the humanities not being able to bring revenue to a state or a university, which, in a time of capital campaigns, shrinking state and federal appropriations, budget cuts, and increased costs to compete for students and faculty, seems a nice pipe dream. Fish's argument is that students and practitioners of the humanities learn or perform a craft, no less or more important than scientists, engineers, or statisticians. He calls the humanities a "business." To attach to them the mission of saving or elevating souls, transforming behavior, or instilling wise counsel that will convert profane human relations into sacred models just misses the reality of its endeavors within the mundane workspace of the contemporary university.

Now let us go to one of the comments in the *New York Times* blog posted in response to Fish's essay. T. Trent writes:

Pretty easy to say when you're one of the people who never once had to ask this particular question in order to earn a living teaching humanities. I'm reading this after 2:30 am because I just picked up four sections of temp-work civilization courses late, late last week. They start tomorrow afternoon. In another city. But, hey, thanks for high-fiving my task: after a dozen hours of trying to shovel Cicero et al. into four syllabi for approximately $8 an hour with no benefits, or, in other words, half of what I earned in construction two decades ago, before I got my Ph.D., I needed a good laugh. And it would be self-centered to wish for more than that.[6]

Trent's irritation is palpable but instructive in that it also focuses on matters of competence, business, and impossible expectations, albeit from a completely different perspective than Fish's. Fish rejects the notion that the humanities should be entrusted with the responsibility to ennoble. Trent does not even see the opportunity for this responsibility, and furthermore resents Fish's preaching from on high that we should not be expected to preach from on high.

So is it the business of the humanities to save us, to remind us of what is true, beautiful, and noble? Are humanities professors our ministers in a secular age? Can we still learn how best to live from the death of Socrates? Should petulant Achilles, wandering Odysseus, or angst-ridden Hamlet be our models? Or do we, like Trent, shovel Cicero, lift iambs, tote spondees, and patch enough together to get us through the next mortgage payment? Is our compass broken, and, if not, can the humanities still point to true North?

Universities have moved from a fixed theocratic curriculum taught by a faculty of generalists to the promotion of secular humanism in a diverse curriculum taught by research specialists to a skepticism of all foundations in both research and teaching. The quest for clarity sometimes becomes obfuscated in jargon-ridden redundancies that celebrate tolerance by limiting debate and that promote equality by denying the rigor of distinction. Humanities has cramped itself in uncomfortable corners premised on following the same research goals of the sciences, yet being unable to generate the research dollars for which university administrators value the sciences. Many students no longer come to our classes seeking the meaning of life; they come to fulfill a requirement for graduation and barely tolerate our attempts to push them out of their comfort zones because our salaries demonstrate such fuss is counterproductive.

Fish tells us we are practitioners of our craft, nothing more, but as such are absolved from the financial obligations of other practitioners of our craft. His respondent is driven by his financial obligations and disparages former deans like Fish for having little grasp of the life of the itinerant instructor with no time for scholarship or for the contemplative life that is its prerequisite. He is a little like the student who wants to get on with life, which means getting on with the dream of financial security. Socrates is interesting, but look at his clothes. Willy Loman, after all, is worth more dead than alive, so what can he teach me? And Macbeth's ambition just got him a crazy wife with a cleanliness fetish. What kind of model for a power couple is that? Getting a Ph.D. ought to give Fish's respondent something better than working construction did. It hasn't, and he resents Fish, whose Ph.D. has, and the educational realities that force him to dispense Cicero like so much gravel and tar on the cracked roadways of our public universities.

In *A Room of One's Own*, Virginia Woolf describes a group of Oxbridge professors:

Many were in cap and gown; some had tufts of fur on their shoulders; others were wheeled in bath-chairs; others, though not past middle age, seemed creased and crushed into shapes so singular that one was reminded of those giant crabs and crayfish who heave with difficulty across the sand of an aquarium. As I leant against the wall the University seemed a sanctuary in which are preserved rare types which would soon be obsolete if left to fight for existence on the pavement of the Strand.[7]

Although ludicrous, this description does not wander far from the clichéd anti-intellectual rhetoric that circulates in state legislatures during hearings on higher education appropriations. Such rhetoric feeds and is fed by public distrust born primarily from misunderstanding over the differences between the university workplace and most other workplaces. This distrust flourishes in an era of economic constraints and corporate downsizing, which increasingly attaches worth to products readily identifiable as useful while zealously excising the cumbersome and the inapplicable. Since the humanities, traditionally the cornerstone of liberal education, increasingly have been targeted as suspicious and, worse, irrelevant, those of us who write and teach in this area increasingly find ourselves tossed on "the pavement of the Strand." It is time we learned to survive there.

For the humanities to protect its future, a more substantive turn in its public engagement mission and practice is essential. Its practitioners need to do a better job explaining how their educational activities include and benefit the broad social as well as the scholarly community and, yes, how they contribute to economic vibrancy through the production of better informed workers and citizens with enhanced critical thinking and communication skills in a knowledge-based economy. More active participation in that community would seem a good first step. Recognizing that the sanctuary of the university depends on the goodwill and positive perception of those who support it might help elevate that support and guard against obsolescence.

Given the adversarial rhetoric about the humanities, what we have not done as well as we might, especially since humanities scholars are those who are trained in rhetoric, is to adequately defend ourselves. We often take reactive positions instead of setting the stage for the debate. We often adopt the methodologies and terminology of other disciplines we perceive as being in favor rather than assert creatively our own skills as

interrogators and wordsmiths. And, most alarmingly, we have not done
the job of connecting with broader constituencies, of translating our work
and our mission so they make sense and resonate with the general public,
of demonstrating our fundamental place in helping to make the personal
and the collective more fulfilling intellectually, spiritually, economically,
culturally, and politically. We need to better communicate our history
lessons and show how the philosophical underpinnings of our founding
documents, the ramifications of which influence our daily and long-term
security and capacity as citizens, are seeded by the humanities and find
their expression in the humanities moments that pervade our lives. Since
the grand challenges and questions of our time require multiple perspectives and deeply contextualized solutions, we must insist on bringing a
humanities lens to bear on their solutions.

Yet a perceptual dichotomy and hierarchy between and in what we
call pure research and public humanities still persists in university hiring,
salary and research awards, and tenure and promotion practices. The job
market is increasingly constrained, yet chairs of dissertation committees
continue to try to replicate themselves via their graduate students, while
the prospects for such replication are at best diminished and at worst nil.
And the digital advances enabling broad and creative dissemination of
scholarship, pedagogy, and intellectual conversations that resonate in the
public sphere are only now creeping into the realm of what is deemed
marginally acceptable in the holy sanctuary of distinguished work. For
all the accusations that they are the bastions of neo-Marxist corruption, universities remain among the most conservative institutions in
our society.

Assessment of quality and success persists as an increasingly conten-
tious yet ubiquitous aspect of academic life. While some form of external
critique or peer review is inherent in virtually every field of humanistic
inquiry, increasing demands by accreditation boards, trustees, funding
organizations, legislatures, and government agencies for stronger and
more quantitative reporting of "outcomes" have produced much conster-
nation. The *Humanities Indicators* published by the American Academy
of Arts and Sciences have provided useful information, but the extent and
manner of their implementation are not yet clear. Academic Analytics has
become the go-to source for assessment of institutional and individual
faculty rankings that largely determine admission into the Association
of American Universities as well as provostian assessments for resource

allocations, yet its understanding of humanities impacts often lags behind and is configured by the paradigms for the sciences.

Furthermore, the means for assessing digital and collaborative research often are vexed, or at least lacking continuity, in most institutional contexts. Also, the advanced research that typically supports ambitious projects in public humanities is sometimes in tension with these projects in terms of audience and impact. Finally, the changing landscapes of scholarly communication have contributed to a sense that assessment metrics and methodologies need serious rethinking.

Questions to be considered in this discussion might involve the following:

1. What kind of time frame offers an accurate assessment of impact?
2. How do we blend qualitative and quantitative assessments usefully?
3. How do we best assess digital, public, and collaborative humanities projects?
4. How do we effectively assess emerging alternative publication venues like web-based publication and open source?
5. How might public humanities be integrated with programs of pure research?
6. What is the value of liberal arts to contemporary university education, and how do we measure its long-term success in life?

Digital humanities and open access have created pathbreaking opportunities for collaboration, dissemination, and reshaping presentation and influence. While the science community generally has quickly accepted open access, seeing it as a means to disseminate its work more expeditiously, especially regarding crucial and immediate concerns, the humanities have lagged behind, perpetuating the two-cultures dichotomy.

Much of the resistance to open access in the humanities has stemmed from a reliance on traditional ideas of peer review, although many forget that double-blind peer review emerged largely in the 1950s and somehow scholarship survived without it before then. This gatekeeper method has not been without its issues, most significantly a perpetuation of sameness in the name of standards. Open access peer review extends the number of commentators, potentially opening the work to fresh considerations from multiple viewpoints while launching a more extended and participatory conversation that still might yield to some circumscribed hierarchy of decision makers but potentially gets ideas into a broader audience quickly, a significant consideration when we are dealing with the crucial grand challenges of contemporary life.

Martin Eve and Kathleen Fitzpatrick have studied this question and posed intriguing alternatives in their books. Publishers are beginning experimental forays into alternative processes. For example, University of California Press has Luminos, an open-source experiment for book publication, which is causing publishers to rethink the traditional means of monograph review and dissemination. Such a model offers the potential

> to exponentially increase the visibility and impact of scholarly work by making it globally accessible and freely available in digital formats. Costs are covered up front through subventions, breaking down barriers of access at the other end—for libraries and for individual readers anywhere in the world. Open access provides the framework for preserving and reinvigorating monograph publishing for the future through sharing costs between all parties who benefit from publication—author or institution, publisher, and libraries. In this model no one entity carries the whole burden, making it sustainable for the long haul. The selection and review processes remain the same as in a traditional program; the same exacting criteria and peer review standards apply.[8]

While one might cite the economic concerns about the fragility of university press budgets and the resultant limited runs of scholarly books, the intensified competition for acceptance of manuscripts, and the pressures on tenure and promotion considerations, early evidence indicates a 20 percent elevation in sales of university press books first offered via open access.

Just as digital humanities projects and web-based publication are forcing universities to rethink tenure and promotion requirements, alternative publication venues like open source will continue to compel us to stretch our imaginations and our bureaucracies to accommodate changes that come naturally both to a technologically enhanced culture and to an intellectually vibrant and interdisciplinary scholarly community. Further, the elitist disdain for work that engages the public domain must take a backseat to the necessity—rhetorical, ethical, and for the sake of survival—to translate the impact of our inquiries within both the esoteric communities of experts as well as the profound intersections where broad ideas touch everyday pleasures and struggles.

Accessibility of both the impact and the language of humanities scholarship to the general public remains a vexed issue and a barrier to countering the prevailing economic myopia used to promote STEM and business studies to the detriment of the humanities. The American Historical Association has spearheaded approaches to broadening graduate curricula so that students have options other than the rapidly shrinking tenure-track route. These include the capacity to write accessibly and to communicate succinctly and effectively the value of historical research. In doing so, they are returning to their roots. In his 1931 presidential address to the AHA, Carl Becker said, "Research will be of little import except in so far as it is translated into common knowledge. . . . The history that lies inert in unread books does no work in the world."[9]

Similarly the National Humanities Center has launched a podcast series in which its resident fellows elucidate their research in fifteen-minute conversations with which an exponentially widening audience has engaged.[10] The Center's *Humanities Moments* project also reaches diverse constituencies of the population who share their recognition of how transformative personal moments in their lives connect to texts, issues, and events directly linked to the humanities.[11] By emphasizing the process of discovery rather than the ultimate product, *Humanities Moments* becomes an understandable scholarly tool easily repurposed for pedagogical applications and for translating the myriad ways by which we solve complex problems in relatable personal terms.

When we confront injustice, our greatest historical moments and transformations in terms of individual heroism and communal coalescence in defense of equality have occurred: "When in the Course of human events it becomes necessary for one people to dissolve the political bands which have connected them with another and to assume among the powers of the earth, the separate and equal station to which the Laws of Nature and of Nature's God entitle them, a decent respect to the opinions of mankind requires that they should declare the causes which impel them to the separation." In an eloquent, poetic, clearly substantiated argument, the Declaration of Independence, an essential document in the great tradition of the humanities, interrogates with power and precision what has rendered the situation in 1776 intolerable in terms of the basic principles of human empowerment and human community, articulating a necessary opposition that would find fruition in that grand bridging document, the Constitution: "We the people, in order to form a more perfect union, establish justice, insure domestic tranquility, provide for the common defence, promote the general welfare, and secure the blessings of liberty to ourselves and our posterity, do ordain and establish this Constitution for the United States of America."[12]

To celebrate the complexity that is at the heart of democracy and to celebrate as well the bridging, the knitting together of contradictions that the humanities embody both in its texts and, just as important, in its application to the most profound junctures of daily life, requires a public recognition that, in our darkest and most troubled moments as well as in those moments of intense joy and revelation, as individuals and as communities, as a people whose deepest bond rests in our embrace rather than in a shunning of diversity, it is the humanities moments in our personal lives and in our collective experiences that teach us best who we are and what we might be. In his great poem about the Irish uprising, "Easter 1916," W. B. Yeats writes, "A terrible beauty is born." This convergence of opposites, how within the troubled flames of historical events we forge insight that demands a reckoning, resounds again and again in the interstices of the humanities moments that populate the crucial connections and compassionate stretches we are called upon to make if our better natures are to endure.

Shakespeare's Sonnet 65, about the ravages of time and the poet's struggles to pen immortal lines in the face of this mortality, offers a similar oppositional move in its initial quatrain:

> Since brass, nor stone, nor earth, nor boundless sea
> But sad mortality o'er-sways their power,
> How with this rage shall beauty hold a plea,
> Whose action is no stronger than a flower?

How with this rage shall beauty hold a plea? I wish to conclude with a few examples of humanities moments that penetrate rage with beauty, that channel our justifiable pain and outrage into actions that sustain and ennoble.

First a debate that, unlike the one between the pope and the rabbi, is by no means silent. On July 13, 2013, George Zimmerman was acquitted in Florida in the shooting death of Trayvon Martin. That evening, three thousand miles away, in Oakland, California, Alicia Garza took to Facebook and posted "A Love Letter to Black People," which included the phrase "Black Lives Matter." Her close friend Patrisse Cullors, who lives in L.A., started sharing this message and others with her friends online, attaching the hashtag #blacklivesmatter. The following day, the two friends spoke about how they might organize a campaign to "make sure we are creating a world where black lives actually do matter." They reached out to a third friend, Opal Tometi, in New York, and the three women set up Tumblr and Twitter accounts where they encouraged users to share stories of why #blacklivesmatter.

This form of hashtag activism gained a strong internet following over the next few months. Then, in August 2014, when Michael Brown was killed by a police officer in Ferguson, Missouri, and protests broke out, the three women and their network helped organize a "freedom ride" as a part of the #blacklivesmatter campaign. More than five hundred people signed up from eighteen cities across the country—and when they arrived in Ferguson, they discovered that there were already protestors carrying banners and chanting the words "Black Lives Matter."

In the intervening months, as media attention began to focus on police violence and the deaths of unarmed black men, the movement grew exponentially, catalyzing young activists, significantly influencing the political campaigns of presidential candidates Bernie Sanders and Hillary Clinton, as well as drawing negative attention from Donald Trump, and by January 2015 the movement had achieved such widespread impact that the American Dialect Society declared #blacklivesmatter their Word of the Year.

There also is the story of Marcia Chatelain, associate professor of history at Georgetown University. Her own response to the events in Ferguson was to create more opportunities for humanities moments in the classroom—to help teachers and students understand the events in Ferguson. As she notes, Michael Brown was shot just two days before he would have begun his freshman year at Vatterott College. In honor of him and in sympathy with her teaching colleagues across the nation, she decided to reach out to educators via Twitter and ask them to commit their first day of classes to talking about Ferguson. She also asked them to suggest a book, an article, a film, a song, a piece of artwork, or an assignment that spoke to some aspect of the Ferguson events, using the hashtag #FergusonSyllabus.

The response was overwhelming, with thousands of tweets and retweets and contributions ranging from a children's book about living with someone with PTSD to maps of St. Louis's school desegregation, from James Baldwin's essay "A Talk to Teachers" to Nina Simone's song "Mississippi Goddam." A community of educators came together, via the internet, across disciplines and from every corner of the country to help each other and their students from preschool to postdoctoral seminars gain a deeper understanding of the national crisis that was centered in the suburbs of St. Louis.

The Black Lives Matter movement is full of humanities moments having originated and explosively grown through social media. The movement has used these platforms to share stories, disseminate powerful video and still images, and facilitate community dialogue about ideas. It also has served as the primary means for organizing direct action, countering official narratives, and debunking media accounts. The power of story, of narrative, that produces empathy and channels outrage into effective action for social justice is woven into the fabric of the humanities.[13]

Consider too an earlier historical moment that illuminates bridging via the humanities. On April 4, 1968, Martin Luther King was assassinated. Robert Kennedy arrived in Indianapolis for a planned campaign rally in his bid for the Democratic nomination for president and was informed of King's death. He was advised by police against making the campaign stop, which was in a part of the city considered to be a dangerous ghetto. But Kennedy insisted on going. He arrived to find the people in a celebratory mood, anticipating the excitement of his appearance. He climbed onto the platform and, realizing they did not know of the assassination, broke the news. Against outcries of pain, anger, and frustration, he went on to calm the crowd by quoting Aeschylus. "My favorite poet was Aeschylus," he said. "He once wrote: 'Even in our sleep, pain which cannot forget falls drop by drop upon the heart, until, in our own despair, against our will, comes wisdom through the awful grace of God.'" And he continued, "What we need in the United States is not division; what we need in the United States is not hatred; what we need in the United States is not violence and lawlessness, but is love and wisdom, and compassion toward one another, and a feeling of justice toward those who still suffer within our country, whether they be white or whether they be black."[14] Indianapolis was the only city in the U.S. with a major African American population that did not burn that night.

Or remember Vedran Smailović, the "cellist of Sarajevo," who regularly played his cello in the National Library and other bombed-out buildings during the Serbian siege of Sarajevo in 1992. Albinoni's Adagio in G Minor would emanate from the strings of Smailović's cello, haunting the air while mortar shells rained down on the city or snipers picked off his friends and neighbors standing in a bread line. Here beauty held a plea, temporarily lifting the prevailing blanket of terror and permitting a peek into an earlier dimension of Sarajevo's history, a reminder of the exquisitely sweet and tender moments that art can attain even against overwhelming barbarity.

Or Paul Kalanithi's memoir of transformation from healing doctor to dying patient in *When Breath Becomes Air*, in which he asks perhaps the basic humanities question: What makes life worth living in the face of death? "The transience of life is the engine of its meaning," Andrew Solomon writes in his review of the book. "Science may provide the most useful way to organize empirical, reproducible data, but its power to do so is predicated on its inability to grasp the most central aspects of human life," Kalanithi argues, "hope, fear, love, hate, beauty, envy, honor, weakness, striving, suffering, virtue." He and his wife make the difficult decision to have a child while knowing he would not live for very long. In their conversations leading up to this decision, his wife asked him "wouldn't it make dying more painful knowing he would be leaving his daughter," and he responded, "Wouldn't it be great if it did."[15]

There are innumerable such examples, and successful public engagement demands that we cite them in order to tell our story in ways that bridge hearts and minds.

How with this rage shall beauty hold a plea? The humanities teach us how. Against all the adversarial rhetoric about the irrelevance of the humanities that pervades policy and sound bites from politicians to concerns of parents about the economic well-being of their liberal arts major children, never have the humanities been more crucial to our sustainability as citizens in a civil society, to the future success of our children and grandchildren, and to discovering and remembering what is most profound and important in our lives.

The mission of the humanities embraces the essence of democracy and a precious underpinning of our American heritage, freedom of thought. It is a mission that should be promoted and respected, no more an extravagance than nourishing food, clean air, or good health care, as sustenance and ministry for quality of life.

As the core of a successful education, a successful life, and a successful civilization, the humanities help us address crucial issues facing us as a people. Absent a humanities perspective, solutions to racial divides, environmental degradation, climate change, immigration, water rights and resources, food consumption, geopolitical cataclysms, and the implementation of new technologies will remain incomplete. Technology cannot assess the multiple masks of evil, the complicated ethics of choice, the pain of loss, the joys of love, or the frustrations and celebrations our yearning to be both human and more than human produce. Technology is premised on answering the hows and the whats, but not the whys. Only in the humanities do we continue to have that conversation despite its often exasperating indeterminacy.

The humanities encourage a culture of rigor, pluralism, innovation, and evidence. As long as these values are maintained in our processes and products, the shape our work takes, the audiences it reaches, and the valuation it receives benefits from a healthy multiplicity and a resistance to static definitions and one-dimensional accountability. We have always been creative in our means of expression and currently are facing an insidious erosion of our raison d'être that feeds into and is fed by the decline of a civil society with an informed and thoughtful public. Our mission includes knowledge production and dissemination not only for the benefit of an esoteric scholarly community but also for the common good.

Notes

1. Greenblatt, *Shakespearean Negotiations*, 1. See also Appiah's essay in this volume for further discussion of this topic.
2. Burke, "Literature as Equipment for Living."
3. Arac, "Peculiarities of (the) English," 194. Nussbaum's *Not for Profit* remains one of the most accessible and compelling arguments for the centrality of the humanities to a democratic culture, using Dewey, Tagore, and Winnicott to consider the importance of imagination, play, and empathy to democratic principles. Helen Small's excellent *The Value of the Humanities* also makes the claim that democracy is strengthened by having a higher level of reasoning available within it. She states, "Mill thought that a university education should have a direct bearing on the 'duties of citizenship,'" and Arnold, Newman, and Ruskin all agreed with him that a university education should involve training in skills that had political application and "the possession of an idea of culture, in which the arts had a guaranteed place, was crucial to the flourishing of the individual and the progress of society" (133).

4. Nussbaum and Glover, *Women, Culture and Development*, 1–2.
5. Fish, "Will the Humanities Save Us?"
6. Trent, comment on Stanley Fish.
7. Woolf, *A Room of One's Own*, 8–9.
8. Luminos website, http://www.luminosoa.org/.
9. Becker, "Everyman His Own Historian," 234.
10. National Humanities Center, *Podcasts*.
11. National Humanities Center, *Humanities Moments*.
12. See Allen's exquisite *Our Declaration*.
13. Thanks to my colleagues Don Solomon, for conveying information about Black Lives Matter responses on social media, and Brooke Andrade, for her help with citations.
14. Kennedy, "Robert F. Kennedy's Speech," 135–36.
15. Kalanithi, *When Breath Becomes Air*, 170,143.

Works Cited

Allen, Danielle. *Our Declaration: A Reading of the Declaration of Independence in Defense of Equality*. New York: Liveright, 2014.

Arac, Jonathan. "Peculiarities of (the) English in the Metanarrative(s) of Knowledge and Power." In *Intellectuals: Aesthetics, Politics, Academics*, edited by Bruce Robbins. Minneapolis: University of Minnesota Press, 1990.

Becker, Carl. "Everyman His Own Historian." *American Historical Review* 37, no. 2 (1932): 221–36.

Burke, Kenneth. "Literature as Equipment for Living." In *Philosophy of the Literary Form: Studies in Symbolic Action*, 293–304. Berkeley: University of California Press, 1973.

Eve, Martin Paul. *Open Access and the Humanities: Contexts, Controversies and the Future*. Cambridge, U.K.: Cambridge University Press, 2015.

Fish, Stanley. "Will the Humanities Save Us?" *New York Times*, January 6, 2008. https://opinionator.blogs.nytimes.com/2008/01/06/will-the-humanities-save-us/.

Fitzpatrick, Kathleen. *Planned Obsolescence: Publishing, Technology, and the Future of the Academy*. New York: NYU Press, 2011.

Greenblatt, Stephen. *Shakespearean Negotiations: The Circulation of Social Energy in Renaissance England*. Oxford: Oxford University Press, 1988.

Kalanithi, Paul. *When Breath Becomes Air*. New York: Random House, 2016.

Kennedy, Robert F. "Robert F. Kennedy's Speech in Indianapolis, April 4, 1968." In *Robert F. Kennedy and the 1968 Indiana Primary*, by Ray E. Boomhower, 135–36. Bloomington: Indiana University Press, 2008.

National Humanities Center. *Podcasts*. http://nationalhumanitiescenter.org/news-and-events/podcasts/.

———. *Humanities Moments*. http://humanitiesmoments.org/.

Nussbaum, Martha. *Not for Profit: Why Democracy Needs the Humanities*. Princeton: Princeton University Press, 2010.

Nussbaum, Martha, and Jonathan Glover. *Women, Culture and Development: A Study of Human Capabilities*. New York: Oxford University Press, 1995.

Shakespeare, William. "Sonnet 65." In *The Complete Sonnets and Poems*, edited by Colin Burrow, 511. Oxford: Oxford University Press, 2002.

Small, Helen. *The Value of the Humanities*. Oxford: Oxford University Press, 2013.

Solomon, Andrew. "'The Good Death,' '*When Breath Becomes Air*' and More." *New York Times*, February 8, 2016. https://www.nytimes.com/2016/02/14/books/review/the-good-death-when-breath-becomes-air-and-more.html.

Trent, T. Comment on Stanley Fish, "Will the Humanities Save Us?" *New York Times*, January 7, 2008. https://opinionator.blogs.nytimes.com/2008/01/06/will-the-humanities-save-us/.

Woolf, Virginia. *A Room of One's Own*. San Diego: Harcourt Brace Jovanovich, 1989.

Yeats, W. B. "Easter, 1916." In *The Collected Works of W. B. Yeats*. Vol. 1: *The Poems*, edited by Richard J. Finneran, 180–81. New York: Scribner, 1997.

What Kind of Humanities Do We Want or Need in the Twenty-First Century?

David Castillo and William Egginton

In 1615 the literary juggernaut Miguel de Cervantes published a short theatrical piece, "The Election of the Mayor of Daganzo," as part of the collection *Eight Plays and Eight Interludes Never Performed*.[1] As candidate Humillos (a clever wordplay that suggests both vain pride and smokescreen) campaigns for the highest office in town, a college graduate asks him a left-field question: "Can you even read, Humillos?" The candidate's response is as straightforward as it is priceless: "Certainly not! And no one will be able to say that a single member of my kin would ever apply themselves to learning those chimeras that drive men to the stake and women to houses of ill-repute, [for] I come from old Christian stock."[2]

This passage is but one of the countless zingers that Cervantes directs against the anti-intellectualist fundamentalism of his age. Remarkably, though, we find similar anti-smarts attitudes and pronouncements in political circles today, prompting the *Washington Post* columnist Jennifer Rubin to admonish some of her fellow Republicans, including public officials like Texas governor Rick Perry and Minnesota senator Michele Bachmann, against "the trap of being proudly ignorant." She comments on remarks made by Governor Perry at Liberty University: "Perry came out with a series of 'See how dumb I am?' one-liners. He observed that he needed to pull out a dictionary to see what 'convocation' meant. . . . And then the real howler: He was in the top 10 in a high school class of 13. . . . It's disturbing to see that he thinks being a rotten student and a know-nothing gives one street cred in the GOP."[3] The larger point that Rubin makes in her article is that inside the political bubble of campaign-style politics, anti-elitism is often conflated and confused with anti-smarts.

In light of this, we propose that now, as in Cervantes's own time, the bigger question might not be *What can we do to rescue the arts and the humanities from their alleged crisis?* but rather, *What can the arts and the humanities do to rescue our society from the epidemic of anti-smarts denialism that has taken hold of the public discourse?* We would argue that an engaged and engaging humanities can help us break through the walls of the media bubble that treats intellectualism with impatience and suspicion, while offering cover to the special interests invested in ignoring or denying such uncomfortable realities as global warming and structural injustice.

Getting back to Cervantes, reading his powerful diagnoses of his time and place in such works as *The Mayor of Daganzo*, *The Stage of Wonders*, and *Don Quixote*, among many others, in the context of self-reflective humanities classes can help us recognize our "glass cage"—in Nicholas Carr's evocative language—and possibly fight back against the imminent danger of anti-intellectual denialism. In fact, Cervantes's comedic lessons on denialism are not lost in the political comedy of our own day. The anti-intellectualism that we see in conservative political circles has provided a steady source of material to satirists such as Jon Stewart and Stephen Colbert. The success of *The Colbert Report*, in particular, was built on a constant mockery of this "Intelligence is suspect" motto, which is often accompanied by the "I can make my own reality" attitude that has become pervasive among conservative media pundits, from Rush Limbaugh and Glenn Beck to Sean Hannity and Bill O'Reilly.

What we call today's *medialogy* promises it will give us the total reality we always knew was there but couldn't access. This is consistent with modern fundamentalism. If early-modern theology emphasized the ineffability of God, modern fundamentalism puts God's will in our hands. The answer to "What would Jesus do?" is "Whatever I believe."

Colbert makes this point very effectively during an interview with John Sexton, president of New York University and the author of *Baseball as the Road to God: Seeing beyond the Game*. Sexton explains, "The key that I am trying to get at in this book is the fact that what we assume we should be doing is searching for meaning . . . but frequently the real meaning of life can't be put in cognitive terms. It's, this is a word I use in my book and in the course, it's ineffable, it can't be reduced to words; we experience it the way we know we are in love, for example; the way we know that life has meaning beyond the obvious." Colbert's tongue-in-cheek response to Sexton's circular argument hits the nail on the head: "I like that; I like that ineffable thing, because then I get to say something is true and then go 'I can't explain it, I am right, though.' I am ineffable about everything."[4] While the ineffable truth of the world used to be guarded by the Church, now the truth is mine; the truth is whatever I believe. Simply put: before, God was ineffable; now, I am ineffable. This is the key to understanding modern fundamentalism.

In his 2016 State of the Union address, President Obama referenced the space race of the cold war years. The reminder that the United States was first to the moon is not particularly remarkable or surprising in the context of national politics. What is interesting (and from our perspective worthy of commentary) is the context provided by the president and the lessons he wanted us to draw from it. "Sixty years ago, when the Russians beat us into space, we didn't deny Sputnik was up there. We didn't argue about the science, or shrink our research and development budget. We built a space program almost overnight, and twelve years later, we were walking on the moon. . . . If anybody still wants to dispute the science around climate change, have at it."[5]

Remarkably, President Obama's mention of the space race in his final State of the Union address was motivated by a desire to caution the public against the crippling effects of antiscience stances and the cynical denial of such facts as global warming. He then goes on to remind us that democracy is essentially unsustainable "when even basic facts are contested, and we listen only to those who agree with us."[6]

Obama has returned to these issues on several occasions. Here's an example from a commencement speech he delivered at Rutgers University in May 2016: "If you were listening to today's political debate, you might wonder where this strain of anti-intellectualism came from. In politics and in life ignorance is not a virtue. It's not cool to not know what you're talking about. That's not keeping it real or telling it like it is. That's not challenging political correctness. . . . The rejection of facts, the rejection of reason and science, that is the path to decline."[7]

But this is exactly what the twenty-four-hour news cycle has given us: a media bubble that protects us from scientific findings, educated arguments, and inconvenient facts. Our choice of networks is based on whether their programming speaks to us directly, that is, whether the news they cover and their framing of the news justifies and reinforces our own views and opinions. As long as we remain inside the comfort zone provided by Fox News, for example, we hardly have to hear from those who disagree with us or even be exposed to scientific or historical facts that might contradict our sense of the world.

It should be noted that this is not a matter of opinion or perspective. In fact, the standard "modern" concept of reality as fundamentally dependent on perception and communal negotiations, subject to individual and collective opinions, perspectives, and expectations can be traced back to Cervantes's own time. Yet this (early) modern notion of reality is based on the assumption that, although reality may be contested and ultimately ineffable (since only God was thought to have complete knowledge of it), it is nonetheless independent from our partial and wholly inadequate version of it. The aesthetics of *desengaño*, "dis-illusion" or "un-deception" that we associate with the art and literature of Cervantes's time, offers a range of explorations of this notion of reality: from the theologically correct view that entrusts reality to the Church and the king as the representatives of God on Earth to the more nuanced (and potentially dissenting) versions of the author of *Don Quixote,* who repurposes the aesthetics of *desengaño* to invite reflection, not on the theological absolutes (the afterlife as the soul's true awakening from the illusion of earthy existence) but on framing techniques and the conditions of visibility that different media formats impose on reality.[8]

The hero of Cervantes's most famous novel did not see the need to change his mind about what he knew to be castles, giants, and armies just because these things looked like inns, windmills, and herds of livestock. Moreover the legendary knight-errant was convinced that what shone on the barber's head was Mambrino's helmet, even though, on closer inspection, the object looked like and felt like a barber's basin. Likewise "President Bush did not see the need to adjust his convictions about global warming or Iraq's weapons of mass-destruction despite all the evidence to the contrary."[9] Meanwhile Barack Obama would be resoundingly criticized for citing climate change rather than terrorism as the real threat to humanity (which, of course, it is).

Rank-and-file citizens can more comfortably focus on the visible threat of a militant other than on the invisible but far more ubiquitous damage our way of life is inflicting on the planet as a whole. This is why we agree with Slavoj Žižek when he wrote, in the aftermath of the Paris attacks of November 2015, "The greatest victims of the Paris terror attacks will be refugees themselves, and the true winners, behind the platitudes in the style of *Je suis Paris,* will be simply the partisans of total war on both sides. This is how we should *really* condemn the Paris killings: not just to engage in shows of anti-terrorist solidarity but to insist on the simple *cui bono* (for whose benefit?) question."[10] But does it solve the problem to ask *cui bono* when our very notion of reality and the desires it supports remain unchanged? Do we not run into the very problem so eloquently analyzed by Žižek himself when he points out that the structure of ideology today is such that awareness is not enough, that we know very well what we are doing but we do it anyway? Does not the current *medialogy* demand a different response, one that Žižek himself theorized in his very first book, when he argued that the effective step required not merely seeing through the illusion but also realizing how one's desire itself is implicated in that illusion?

Indeed, articulating and arguing for a position can seem fruitless, since today's medialogy is able to package any such position, no matter how urgent, into yet another portable reality, complete with its own interest group, marketing, and product line. It does not escape us that in order for these very lines we are now writing to have any potential impact, we will depend on exactly the same mechanisms provided by the very medialogy we are attempting to elucidate. That said, what is certainly not enough is to double down on truth, as if the ills of today's medialogy were an effect of relativism instead of its opposite, fundamentalism. And if the fundamentalists (at least of the Christian variety) have a mantra, WWJD, "What would Jesus do?" (although we suspect that whatever the historical Jesus would do, it would have very little similarity to what today's fundamentalists think he would do), we prefer to replace that with a mantra of our own: WWCD, or "What would Cervantes do?"

The reason we see Cervantes as a model of humanistic critique is that he developed a special insight into how the media frame not only what we see but what we want to see. And his response was not to deny that reality, not to stake a different claim to truth, but to depict himself, his contemporaries, us, in the act of being formed by that medialogy. By showing us not a different version of the world but how the world can produce so many versions of itself, Cervantes created a form of cultural production, which we now call fiction, which has the power to attune minds to actively *reading reality* as opposed to passively receiving it.

Only a short time after Cervantes, the German mathematician and philosopher Gottfried Leibniz wrote, "If someone looks attentively at more pictures of plants and animals than another person, and at more diagrams of machines and descriptions and depictions of houses and fortresses, and if he reads more imaginative novels and listens to more strange stories, then he can be said to have more knowledge than the other, even if there is not a word of truth in all that he has seen and heard."[11] We believe that Leibniz's words hold a special wisdom. Literature, art, and philosophy have the capacity to teach us to think differently, precisely and especially when they are not captive to a strictly representationalist or objectivist logic. Hence our almost obnoxiously simple yet totally urgent prescription: More humanities!

Reading literature and viewing art and thinking and writing about these experiences is the vital and indispensable foundation for any possible liberation from today's medialogy and the self-destructive traps of desire it engenders. This is not a reductively idealistic prescription, too far removed from the real dangers that threaten us. We know that we are destroying the environment, but we continue to do nothing. Encouraging narrow, technologically and instrumentally oriented education is clearly not solving the problem, and is most likely contributing to it. Global fragmentation continues to rise, and our responses make the situation worse. Current educational practices are clearly doing little to solve these problems either, yet in less time than it takes the oceans to rise a meter, an entire generation could be introduced to the humanities and the practices of interpretation that characterize them. A new generation of people more likely to be reflective, more likely to see how their own desires and actions impact the world, could arise.

We know we are preaching to the choir, but the choir needs to become more strident. The choir needs to stop being embarrassed about its interests and methods, stand up proudly, and insist that there is no such thing as an adequate education, at any level, that does not include humanistic inquiry. The humanities are not a luxury, not just a shiny patina to make our bleak lives prettier; they are vital to our very survival as a species. Without them we will continue on our present course, with our own individual reality in hand, self-contained fiefdoms in an empire of solitude, doomed, as in the prophetic closing words of García Márquez's great novel, never to have a chance on this earth again.

We would be justified in asking just how this kind of mobilization in support of the humanities is likely to work, when more than two thirds of the teaching force is overworked and ineligible for tenure, when political leaders, parents, and even students themselves seem to have decided that

STEM and STEM alone is the pathway to a successful future. But there are many ways forward, and as directors of humanities institutes at our respective universities we are both committed to pursuing all those we can. To take one example, at Johns Hopkins University, where 60 percent of each entering class indicates an intent to follow the premedical track, the Alexander Grass Humanities Institute hosts a new major called Medicine, Science, and Humanities. The major, which is only in its third year, already has put more science students in humanities classrooms than any previous effort. At SUNY Buffalo we are starting an annual event series we are calling "Humanities to the Rescue," focused on the need for the humanities to reclaim a central position in public debates on the big challenges of our time, from climate change and environmental justice to the rise of racism and misogyny and the crisis of democracy around the world. This is part of multiyear public humanities programming that kicked off in fall 2017 with a Humanities Festival on the theme "Environments," a cross-institutional collaboration involving several local and regional institutions, including Buffalo State, Canisius College, Niagara University, and Humanities New York. Climate change science and the politics of denialism, environmental justice and forward paths at the local and global scales are among the topics for discussion, as we try to encourage meaningful conversations between the humanistic and scientific disciplines, the arts, activist groups, public policy makers, and the public at large.

For us today, the catastrophe that is just around the corner and that we nevertheless dutifully ignore, the cataclysm that is already uprooting and dispossessing legions of the world's poor and promises a future of ever-greater waves of refugees around the planet, is climate change. As Naomi Klein argues in her indictment of neoliberalism's inherent conflict with the climate, *This Changes Everything*, "Faced with a crisis that threatens our survival as a species, our entire culture is continuing to do the very thing that caused the crisis, only with an extra dose of elbow grease behind it."[12]

What is certain is that we are already headed, inexorably, for a future with more vicious storms, flooding, droughts, heat waves, and blizzards, with the economic and human tolls disproportionately affecting those nations and people who have least contributed to the problem through their greenhouse emissions and least benefited from the industrial development that produces those emissions. We are already, that is, locked into a future with at least an average increase of two degrees Celsius, and are more likely looking at a scenario in which average temperatures are four degrees higher by the century's end.[13] As a former director of the Tyndall Centre for Climate Change Research says, an increase of four degrees Celsius is "incompatible with any reasonable characterization of an organized, equitable, and civilized global community."[14]

Here is a tiny portion of Klein's chilling (pardon the irony) description of a planet whose average temperature is four degrees higher than today's, for which "even the best case scenario is likely to be calamitous":

> Four degrees of warming would raise the global sea levels by 1 or possibly even 2 meters by 2100 (and would lock in at least a few additional meters over future centuries). This would drown some island nations such as the Maldives and Tuvalu, and inundate many coastal areas from Ecuador and Brazil to the Netherlands to much of California and the northeastern United States, as well as huge swaths of South and Southeast Asia.[15]

She goes on to describe massive crop losses, famine, killer heat waves, and megastorms, then ends on the cheery note that, according to many models, we are on a trajectory for even greater warming than four degrees. Why are we so invested, then, in averting our eyes and doing nothing? Her answer is that because the changes needed are so profound, all the combined resources of the world's entrenched elites are marshaled against anyone succeeding in making those changes:

> We are stuck because the actions that would give us the best chance of averting catastrophe—and would benefit the vast majority—are extremely threatening to an elite minority that has a stranglehold over our economy, our political process, and most of our major media outlets. That problem might not have been insurmountable had it presented itself at another point in our history. But it is our great collective misfortune that the scientific community made its decisive diagnosis of the climate threat at the precise moment when those elites were enjoying more unfettered political, cultural, and intellectual power than at any point since in the 1920s.[16]

Indeed, the elites' influence over the media is key to understanding why the world blissfully goes on spinning the rope with which it will hang itself, while the same elites hunker down in estates paid for by profits they make selling that rope at a handsome markup. But it is not merely a matter (although it certainly is that as well) of buying up news outlets and funding think tanks like Heartland and the Cato Institute to cook up "scientific" studies and spread climate skepticism. Something else is at stake when such large portions of the world's populations can be guided into ignoring a reality that their very lives depend on their not ignoring.

In current popular culture, our fantasies often incorporate these notions in apocalyptic scenarios in which our treatment of the *world as resource* combined with the kind of denialism that goes along with what we call *reality entitlement* (I am entitled to my own reality) produce catastrophic consequences for the human race. James Patterson's apocalyptic bestseller *Zoo*, with its spinoff CBS TV series, provides a good illustration of this paradox. In the novel, "cell phone radiation is somehow cooking the ambient environmental hydrocarbons in a way we've never seen before—morphing them into a chemical that animals are picking up as a pheromone." The result is widespread zombie-like behavior in animals that brings humanity to the brink of extinction. Against this established fact and with the human apocalypse on the horizon unless we can stop our use of cell phones, cars, and so on, people will just continue to use the technology that's killing them, simply because "it is the way of life, the way of the world."[17]

The explanation for this apparently willful ignorance lies in today's medialogy. For the dominant economic model we call neoliberalism, the world consists of *resources* that agents, mainly individuals, but also collectives of individuals like corporations and states, use and manage. When the entire world is conceived as an ultimately expendable (albeit at the cost of our survival) resource, this is when the concept of sustainability comes into play.

Obviously the idea behind sustainability is a noble one; indeed, if the proscriptions of sustainability were or had been until now followed, then the catastrophe of an ever-warming planet could be averted. But the dark side of sustainability is the insight it gives us into how the world is situated in the current medialogy: the world, once the transcendent, ineffable ground of appearances, has been relegated to the status of the copies—just one more, if greater, resource among equals. In Heidegger's famous formulation, like the great Danube whose waters have been locked behind a grid of hydroelectric dams, the world itself has been converted into a standing reserve.[18]

But what allows a ground as fundamental as the entire world to be subsumed by the logic of resources is how our medialogy frames reality. Neoliberalism's all-out focus on the market agency of the individual as consumer simply has no room for noncommodities. This is why the policy recommendations in the discourse of sustainability often come dressed as commodity fetishes: carbon credits that wealthy companies or nations can purchase to offset their polluting ways, much as wealthy Catholics in the sixteenth century might have purchased indulgences to offset the pleasures of their sinful lives.

In a sense, the language of sustainability is the shadow indicator of our very inability to imagine any alternatives to capitalism as a global economic system; for the current medialogy, reality itself has the form of a commodity, which makes it all the easier for the elites controlling governments and markets to package and sell their own versions. As Colbert's pundit persona so famously put it, reality has a well-known liberal bias.

This explains how a well-regarded architect and theorist in Italy like Giovanni Galli, in pointing to sustainability as the potential symbolic form of the twenty-first century, himself adopts the rhetorical stance of a climate change denier. He grounds his critical stance vis-à-vis the sustainability movement on the ostensibly philosophical, even hermeneutic argument that the seemingly urgent need for a politics of sustainability presupposes a static vision of being, one in which values are intrinsic to nature as opposed to invented by men. Understood this way, he argues, "products of a fossil origin (oil, coal, gas) don't have a value in themselves, but only insofar as they are made useful by and for the labor of mankind." This much may seem obvious, but the conclusion he draws is eye-opening: "From this perspective, as the economist Julian Simon has argued, resources are inexhaustible."[19] What Galli doesn't mention is that Simon was employed by the Cato Institute until his death in 1998, an institute financed in large part by big business, and specifically big oil, with the purpose of producing policy papers in support of those industries. What underlies such thinking, however, is both more specific and much, much more fundamental. The inexhaustibility of resources in this model is linked directly to the ungrounded nature of value.

Climate denial, the self-annihilating, apocalyptic engine of our times, expresses in its purest form the power of our medialogy. Just as when the substance of a nation—once the ineffable thing to which symbolic copies (states) referred to—is turned into a hollow shell and shaken by ethnic substances, warring tribal alliances, or new racisms, in the new medialogy the entire world, once the ineffable ground of all existence, reveals itself as just one more resource. The market society effectively sidelines reality, turning its naming rights over to the highest bidder.

In 2016 political pundits of all persuasions struggled to explain the unprecedented appeal of Donald Trump. And yet what Trump promised his boisterous audiences is no different from what the media culture of the market society is already promising them every day: *the right to be unlimited*—if we can borrow from the phrasing of the familiar Sprint/iPhone commercial. In this sense, Trump's populist message is simply an updating of the theme of American exceptionalism for the new millennium and a reissuing of the American dream at a global and unlimited scale. He is going to build a wall on the U.S. southern border to keep rapists out, to prevent them from taking our women, and Mexico is going to pay for it; he is going to stop China from stealing our riches and reclaim our markets around the world; he is going to bomb the hell out of ISIS and take the oil . . . In other words, he is going to make sure no one steals your enjoyment rights; he is going to deliver to you the keys to the world. This is nothing more than what our market society already promises on a regular basis: our (American) right to unlimited enjoyment in a world that's ours to own. Turning President Kennedy's legendary charge on its head, Trump would be saying, "Ask not what you can do for your country, but what your country, and the world, can do for you!"

There's no nuance in Trump's messaging, no analysis, no insight into historical realities, no talk of structural inequalities, social justice, global warming; there's only a promise "to make America great again" so that you can enjoy your birthright: America's Exceptionalism Unlimited! This is ultimately what the new market fundamentalism looks like: You have the right to your own reality! In other words, reality is simply your entitlement as an American.

Back to the question we posed at the beginning: What kind of humanities do we want or need in the twenty-first century? In the all-pervasive market society, it is not enough to defend the value of the humanities in an increasingly corporatized university. Instead the humanities can and should go on the offensive to denounce the blinding effects of market fundamentalism and poke holes in the media-framed reality that's coextensive with it.

Notes

1. Part of this chapter appears in our coauthored book *Medialogies*.

2. "No, por cierto, ni tal se probara en mi linaje haya persona de tan poco asiento, que se ponga a aprender esas quimeras, que llevan a los hombres al brasero, y a la mujeres a la casa llana . . . con ser yo cristiano viejo." Cervantes, "La elección de los alcaldes de Daganzo," in *Entremeses*, 154–55 (our translation).

3. Rubin, "GOP Should Not Fall."

4. *The Colbert Report*, "Interview with John Sexton."

5. Obama, "2016 State of the Union Address."

6. Ibid.

7. Fieldstadt, "President Obama Attacks."

8. Castillo and Egginton, *Medialogies*, 169–86.

9. Castillo, "Don Quixote and Political Satire," 175.

10. Žižek, "In the Wake of Paris Attacks."

11. Leibniz, *New Essays*, 355.

12. Klein, *This Changes Everything*, 2.

13. Should the provisions of the Paris Agreement produced by the 2015 United Nations Climate Change Conference in Paris be ratified and adhered to, there is a chance that temperatures could be held to less than two degrees Celsius above preindustrial levels.

14. Klein, *This Changes Everything*, 13.

15. Ibid., 13.

16. Ibid., 15.

17. Patterson and Ledwidge, *Zoo*, 268, 357.

18. Heidegger, "The Question concerning Technology," 325.

19. Galli, *Sostenibilità e Potere*, 19, our translation.

Works Cited

Carr, Nicholas. *The Glass Cage: Automation and Us*. New York: Norton, 2014.

Castillo, David. "Don Quixote and Political Satire: Cervantine Lessons from Sacha Baron Cohen and Stephen Colbert." In *Approaches to Teaching Cervantes's Don Quixote*, edited by James Parr and Lisa Vollendorf, 171–77. New York: MLA, 2015.

Castillo, David, and William Egginton. *Medialogies: Reading Reality in the Age of Inflationary Media*. London: Bloomsbury, 2017.

Cervantes, Miguel de. *Don Quijote de la Mancha*. 2 vols. Edited by John Jay Allen. Madrid: Cátedra, 1998.

———. *Entremeses*. Edited by Nicholas Spadaccini. Madrid: Cátedra, 1994.

The Colbert Report. "Interview with John Sexton." March 7, 2013. http://www.cc.com/video-clips/uldxcb/the-colbert-report-john-sexton.

Fieldstadt, Elisha. "President Obama Attacks Trump's Wall and 'Anti-Intellectualism' in Rutgers Commencement Speech." *NBC News*. May 15, 2016.

http://www.nbcnews.com/politics/barack-obama/president-obama-attacks
-trump-s-wall-anti-intellectualism-rutgers-commencement-n574361.
Galli, Giovanni. *Sostenibilità e Potere*. Genova: Sagep, 2015.
Heidegger, Martin. "The Question concerning Technology." In *Basic Writings*,
edited by David Krell. New York: HarperCollins, 2003.
Klein, Naomi. *This Changes Everything: Capitalism vs. the Climate*. New York:
Simon and Schuster, 2014.
Leibniz, Gottfried. *New Essays on Human Understanding*. Translated and edited
by Peter Remnant and Jonathan Bennett. Cambridge, U.K.: Cambridge Uni-
versity Press, 1982.
Obama, Barack. "2016 State of the Union Address." *Washington Post*. Accessed
December 28, 2016. http://www.washingtonpost.com/wp-srv/politics
/documents/Obama_SOTU_2011_transcript.html.
Patterson, James, and Michael Ledwidge. *Zoo*. New York: Century, 2012.
Rubin, Jennifer. "GOP Should Not Fall into the Trap of Being Proudly Igno-
rant." *Washington Post,* September 14, 2011. https://www.washingtonpost
.com/blogs/right-turn/post/gop-should-not-fall-into-the-trap-of-being-proudly
-ignorant/2011/03/29/gIQA1glFSK_blog.html?utm_term=.657b48a40237.
Žižek, Slavoj. "In the Wake of Paris Attacks the Left Must Embrace Its Radical
Western Roots: Žižek Responds to His Critics on the Refugee Crisis." *In These
Times,* November 16, 2015. http://inthesetimes.com/article/18605.

The Humanities in the World: A Field Report

Mariët Westermann

My essay title will seem absurdly comprehensive. Still, current conditions of the humanities, and of "the world" taken in several senses, make this header appropriate for a brief field report on risks and opportunities for the humanistic disciplines today. The essay has three parts of different but interconnected character.

First, I will briefly disentangle the question of a crisis *within* the humanities in the academy, which has arisen around whether and where these fields continue to be studied. Because some of the concerns about such a crisis focus on the question of the relevance of the humanities in our world today, I then turn to the rise of the public humanities, a sphere of enterprise often defined as the interface between the academy and the world, or even as a world of action entirely outside the academy.

In the second section, I will discuss two grand challenges in and for the world as a system of sovereign states. I have selected these particular problems because the humanities are well suited to address them on their own methodological terms. The problems are entwined with each other: the first is the long-standing dynamic whereby the state system produces growing numbers of "refugees," which I take as an inclusive term for internally displaced groups, forcibly exiled people, and immigrants seeking socioeconomic security by crossing borders without state sanction and at great physical risk. These groups include millions of stateless, near-stateless, or soon-to-be-stateless people, who can expect only the most tenuous protections from their destination states or have to subsist without political rights whatsoever. The second challenge is the ongoing and relentless violence against the cultural heritage of particular ethnic and/or religious groups by governments, rebel groups, or self-declared political organizations that find expediency in such actions, from the systematic suppression of religious and civic rituals to the spectacular destruction and looting of sites, buildings, and artifacts in order to proclaim an ideology or simply intimidate opposing groups.

These geopolitical challenges make for bleak topics, but in the third section my lens will shift from the humanities in the world to *humanists* in the field. I will offer a report on an institution of cultural heritage and a public humanities project, both of which are deploying humanities methods and resources to make visible the long shadows of history and to foster understanding on the part of majority groups of the histories and cultures they share with minorities in their environments.

The "Crisis" of the Humanities in the World

At the Andrew W. Mellon Foundation, which is dedicated to the humanities, arts, and higher education as engines of human flourishing and diverse and democratic societies, there has rarely been a day since the economic crash of 2008 that a visitor has not asked us what we are going to do about "the crisis of the humanities."[1] In response, most of us who work there have tended to resist this language, not because we have no worries about the humanities or no sympathy for colleagues struggling to make enrollment numbers and handle budget cuts; it is rather that the word "crisis" seems too undifferentiated to diagnose challenges faced by humanists, which are multifaceted, intricately layered, and asymmetrically distributed across the system of higher education.[2]

Here are some of the things we know and do not really know about the humanities today, pulled together with the help of the *Humanities Indicators*, the extremely useful data aggregation website compiled by the American Academy of Arts and Sciences that tracks trends in the humanities.[3] As figures 1 and 2 show, over the past thirty years the production of bachelor's degrees with majors in the humanities first rose, both in number and as a percentage of all majors, to a high of 15 percent in 2005, and then gradually declined to about 12 percent—roughly the same as it was in 1988.[4] Breaking down these numbers into broad disciplinary and professional categories, figure 3 demonstrates that it is mostly the humanities and education that have lost relative ground. The natural sciences, at less than 11 percent, may not look like a big winner, but they are trending up, and if one adds health and medical sciences and engineering, which show similar upward trends, the STEM disciplines

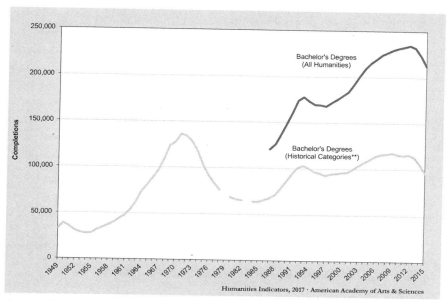

Figure 1. Bachelor's degree completions in the humanities (for full source and context for all figures in this chapter, see http://humanitiesindicators.org)

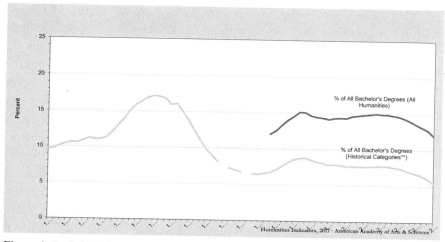

Figure 2. Bachelor's degrees in the humanities as a percentage of all bachelor's degrees

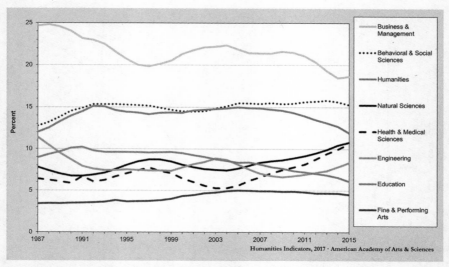

Figure 3. Shares of all bachelor's degrees awarded in selected fields

produce 30 percent of all undergraduate degrees. Whether the downturn pattern for the humanities that we are seeing in the United States will continue is an open question; clearly, there have been significant fluctuations since degrees began to be tracked by major in the 1950s. As with many confounding trends, pronouncements on their "meaning" may be reductive and may have partially positive explanations. For example, some have postulated that women began to turn away from the humanities as the sciences became more welcoming and encouraging of female participation.[5]

Insistent demands for immediate employment outcomes coming out of state legislatures and governors' offices have certainly put great pressure on the humanities in public institutions, but the effects of these attacks on humanities enrollments are not clear yet. In fact, when one looks at humanities degrees as a percentage of all degrees awarded in different types of colleges and universities (fig. 4), public institutions appear to have closed what was in 1987 a 4 percent gap with private institutions in humanities degrees as a share of all the degrees they awarded. These trend lines seem to suggest that the greatest losses of humanities majors have been sustained in private universities and colleges. Public institutions now award twice as many of all bachelor's degrees in the humanities as private not-for-profit universities and colleges (fig. 5).

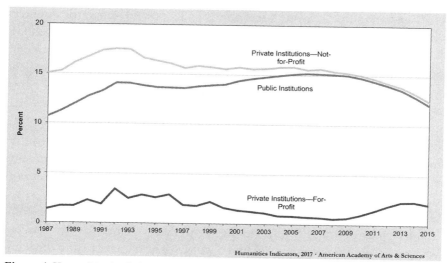

Figure 4. Humanities bachelor's degrees as a percentage of all bachelor's degrees awarded by public versus private institutions

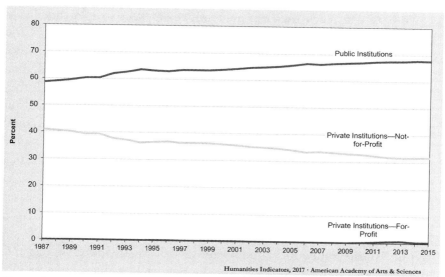

Figure 5. Percentage of all bachelor's degrees in the humanities awarded by public versus private institutions

There are some reasons for optimism. Plenty of humanities courses are not captured in these tallies, such as the ones in professional schools and in new areas of study that have significant humanities components but are not (yet) standardized majors. The two-year community college sector, which enrolls about 40 percent of all American undergraduates, is conferring larger numbers of associate degrees in the humanities than ever before, and the humanities make up the largest share of majors—42 percent (figs. 6 and 7). In this sector, almost all general education requirements are in the humanities. Given that most community college students want to obtain a bachelor's degree, this sector presents a great opportunity to grow humanities enrollments in four-year institutions.[6] Much remains to be done in understanding and optimizing the role that community colleges can play in fostering the humanities, but for the moment we should simply note that the humanities are not "on the run" throughout the sector.

What, then, are we trying to defend when we appeal to a crisis in the humanities? Is it the preservation of a traditional disciplinary structure through departments, majors, and Ph.D. programs? Surely we do need people who can teach the next generation and keep scholarship lively. But preserving the humanities as we have known them since, say, World War II, for their own sake cannot be the whole argument. Are we not also interested in the role of the humanities in supporting a broad, integrated education that can help people acquire the literacies and skills they need for life in the twenty-first century and for full participation in our democracy and economy? If one takes those broader goals into account and notices the humanities action in community colleges and professional schools, the humanities may not be in crisis. Martha Kanter, the former undersecretary for higher education, once told me, "If you are pulled over by a police officer for a traffic infraction, would you not prefer it if she had read some Shakespeare, like *Measure for Measure*?"

Although at the Mellon Foundation we see higher education as the guardian of the humanities broadly construed, we are more interested in how the humanities nurture human flourishing in a diverse democracy than in preserving the precise academic arrangements the humanities have long held in the departmental structures and reward systems of colleges and universities. A revisioning and retooling of how the humanities are taught appears to be in order, and in many places, including the country's leading humanities centers, it is underway. With new articulations among

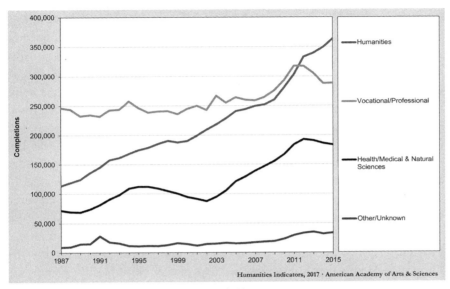

Figure 6. Associate's degree completions by field

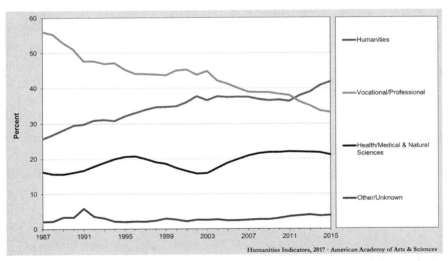

Figure 7. Associate's degree completions in selected fields as a percentage of all associate's degree completions

courses that produce problem-focused pathways through the curriculum, undergraduate education has begun to integrate history, philosophy, languages, literature, the arts, and media to study big questions in consort with the sciences, the social sciences, and the professions.[7] Undergraduate students are highly motivated by coursework in any discipline that helps them bring to bear classroom learning on the problems of creating a more just, equitable, and livable planet. Sorting out how to teach humanity's cultural history in a way that values traditional research capacities but also conveys such social relevance is a challenge for humanities faculty trained in a different moment, but many are trying to take it on.

I see no incongruity between a commitment to, even love of academic scholarship and a call for a regrounding of the humanities in the world around us. This reorientation requires recognition that the humanities inherently concern the cultural record of the world, and that for the humanities to thrive, humanists need to parlay this worldly grounding into publications, courses, collaborative projects, and engagements in the communities outside their campus walls. In this sense, the "world" of my title signals an allegiance to Edward Said's decades-old reminder, in the string of essays published as *The World, the Text, and the Critic* in 1983, that writers and those who write about them never produce a neutral account, that their texts are inevitably embedded in social relations, and that these works bear the marks of that worldliness.[8] At the time, Said was concerned that an overemphasis on creating a professional class of academic critics was separating the humanities too decisively from the world that situates their objects of study. Said wrote about texts, of course, but his arguments extend to the humanities at large. Although historians of art, music, dance, theater, and ritual deal with visual, aural, performative, and material culture, the specificity of physical objects and forms that do aesthetic work through the people that use them obviously requires that these humanists also attend to the worldly grounding of their scholarship. In his essays, Said argued in a dozen different ways that how humanities scholars work with texts as worldly productions has inescapable implications for how we stand in the contemporary world and may imagine its future.

Hannah Arendt, one of the most significant public humanists of the twentieth century, continues to provide a critical touchstone for thinking about the worldly position of humanities research in relation to the present and the future. Our century's violent conflicts, ongoing refugee crises, and challenges to democratic institutions have brought her work back to constant consciousness. While Arendt has long been central to critical theory, history, and legal philosophy, many humanities disciplines, museums, and other organizations of culture appear almost completely unaware of her thought. As she has much to offer cultural memory organizations and heritage thinkers of our time, I will recite her well-known statement on the impossibility of writing history as an oblivious sort of homesickness. From the preface to *The Origins of Totalitarianism*, her magnum opus of 1950:

> We can no longer afford to take that which was good in the past and simply call it our heritage, to discard the bad and simply think of it as a dead load which by itself time will bury in oblivion. The subterranean stream of Western history has finally come to the surface and usurped the dignity of our tradition. . . . And this is why all efforts to escape from the grimness of the present into nostalgia for a still intact past, or into the anticipated oblivion of a better future, are vain.[9]

Many institutions of cultural heritage resist, in whole or in part, working through history in an aware, anti-oblivious mode, even as they dedicate themselves to the preservation of the past—but I am getting ahead of my story.

One way in which universities are seeking to address the crisis of humanities enrollments and to manifest the worldly utility of the humanities in a civically engaged way is within the broad sphere of activity loosely designated *the public humanities*. For the most part, the public humanities movement—for given the level of broadly distributed, intentional activity now captured by the rubric the public humanities have the characteristics of a movement—that brings humanities research into a wider world strikes me as a promising development, but I do want to note a worry about the public humanities as they are commonly understood by administrators and perhaps many faculty members as well. My sense in surveying the field is that public humanities are still too often thought of as a set of translational activities, pursued through tried and true methods of "outreach" that have now been given a different name, rather than as reciprocal interventions that use the methods of the humanities to engage communities in problem solving and that value a community's input into one's humanities practice as a form of research. In this view, the public

humanities are positioned as a collective act of generosity on the part of
scholars, extraneous to their "own work" or that of their institutions.
Few public humanities efforts really address some of the grand challenges
at whose table the humanities have tried to gain a seat, though there
are several outstanding examples, such as the Seminar on Public Engagement and Collaborative Research at the Humanities Center of the City
University of New York Graduate Center. The seminar coordinates more
than forty faculty and Ph.D. students into working groups that conduct
community archival projects and public programs on topics from "public knowledge and the role of media" to "human trafficking and racial
justice." When public humanities programs involve graduate students
and community organizations in such rich, two-way interactions around
worldly issues, one is tempted once and for all to divorce the term "crisis"
from the humanities.

Grand Challenges for the Humanities

However one circumscribes the humanities, they should be deployable
to the needs of any problem of the human condition, as the *human* in
the humanities implies. If that is so, humanists ought to be able to participate in addressing any of the intractable quandaries of our time, from
nuclear disarmament to halting climate change, from producing trade
arrangements that halt the growth in inequality to the responsibility to
protect people at risk of genocide. Humanists should certainly research,
reflect on, and teach about these problems and make productive noise
about them to help hold governments and the international community
accountable. Nevertheless, in the societal sphere the expertise and methods of the humanities may lend themselves better to certain interactions
or problems than others. Some challenges even seem to cry out for the
intervention of humanists.

Two massive geopolitical problems today are not simply matters of
diplomacy and international law but beg for humanities expertise and
methods. The tools and resources provided by a long history of thought,
writing, and curatorship can help inform, educate, and perhaps ameliorate these conditions as well as produce speculative ideas for a better
future. Scholars can do so with the assistance of institutions, besides
their own universities, which already have the public humanities in their

mission—particularly libraries, archives, and museums of art, history, and culture.

The first problem is the question of how sovereign nation-states deal with newcomer populations that have entered without immediate or long-term chances at obtaining legal rights. Current citizens of these states may consider the incoming migrants alien or even threatening to their ways of life. These are the refugees: the stateless or the near-stateless or the always at risk of becoming stateless. The second grand challenge is the destruction of cultural heritage as an instrument of political and civil war. These problems turn out to be entwined in complex ways, as are some solutions to them.

Arendt gave us an insightful and harrowing phenomenological account of the condition of bare humanity that leaves the stateless without legal rights. She wrote from a basis in her experience of stateless exile, showing how this condition deprives human beings of access to elusive "human rights" when there is no political entity to which they can appeal to have such rights enforced:

> The calamity of the rightless is not that they are deprived of life, liberty, and the pursuit of happiness or of equality before the law and freedom of opinion—[human rights] formulas which were designed to solve problems *within* given communities—but that they no longer belong to any community whatsoever. Their plight is not that they are not equal before the law, but that no law exists for them; not that they are oppressed but that nobody wants to oppress them.[10]

While we tend to think of refugees in the way the 1951 UN Convention Relating to the Status of Refugees defines them, as people persecuted by their governments and caught in crossfires of war, Arendt's analysis suggests that many more people are stateless or near-stateless than the waves of refugees from Iraq, Syria, or Myanmar on which the international community is focused at the moment.[11] Undocumented immigrants already in the United States, for example, and those who are on the run from violent conditions or grave economic insecurity in their Central American countries and are hoping to cross the border, live in similar states of legal precarity without safe options of return. If ethnoreligious minorities, such as the remaining Jews of Iran and political dissidents hiding in Cambodian villages, are able to leave their countries, they may

paradoxically prefer a stateless condition that at least keeps potential destination countries from being able to ship them back too easily.

What most of these largely rightless people have in common is the
perception on the part of sovereign governments or their constituents
that they threaten the host country's economic, civic, or political stability,
and that their very refugee status somehow derives from or maps onto a
moral character that must be questionable precisely because they are refugees.[12] Appealing to the "common humanity" of the Syrian refugee and
the undocumented Honduran child appears to have limited effect on state
policies, although governments will sometimes use that rhetoric if they
are inclined to extend legal rights anyway and seek to sway their people.
In the end, the political will and viability of the government of any state
confronted with a potential influx of refugees or economic migrants will
determine their fate—human rights alone are no guarantee of protection.
Because we appear to have a limited capacity for seeing others thrown
upon our shores as our own, finding their practical value for the host
country and its people offers a pragmatic path to seeing displaced people
in a positive light. I will return to this possibility.

The millions of people around the world who live without legal rights
or with the imminent threat of losing them may still belong to their ethnic
or religious communities, but they are not part of a *political* community.
And belonging to a political community—a society—means that having
freedom of *opinion* is not just a matter of being free to think whatever
you want, but of being able to act in consort with others to shape a society of laws. Arendt underscores this:

> The fundamental deprivation of human rights is manifested first and
> above all in the deprivation of a place in the *world* which makes
> opinions significant and actions effective. Something much more fun-
> damental than freedom and justice, which are rights of citizens, is at
> stake when belonging to the community into which one is born is no
> longer a matter of choice, or when one is placed in a situation where,
> unless he commits a crime, his treatment by others does not depend
> on what he does or does not do.[13]

Arendt's razor sharp analysis showed that the political philosophy and
practices of European nation-states after World War I toward minority
populations had caused a massive refugee crisis, and that the continued

logic of the nation-state meant that refugee crises would not simply be resolved by the ending of World War II. She also indicated that political expulsion practices were prepared, aided, and abetted by policies of cultural deracination most fully perfected by the Nazi regime but easily perpetrated by any state with totalitarian tendencies. Oppressive governments have continued to deploy strategies of ethnic debasement and vilification through cultural heritage destruction. The burnings of books and synagogues in the Third Reich have innumerable analogues in atrocities committed in civil and ethnic wars, including the systematic destruction of the arts in Cambodia that accompanied the deaths of more than two million under the Khmer Rouge, the desecration of Sufi Muslim graves in Timbuktu, and the destruction of Tibet's cultural heritage by the Chinese state while one-sixth of the Tibetan population was killed.

In the new, highly localized warfare that has become endemic since the end of the Cold War, attacks on cultural heritage sites, artifacts, and performance and ritual traditions have become battlefield tactics, intended to position a particular ethnic or religious group as too alien to be accommodated by a particular society or religion.[14] Unlike the Nazi government, which denied the atrocities it had committed as enemy propaganda, contemporary perpetrators of cultural heritage destruction often promote their "success" through video and social media. These actions bring multiple benefits to the assaulting group or regime—some traditional and others new. Over the course of history, destruction of sites and artifacts of cultural or political significance has often sent a message of raw power and authority intended to legitimize regimes to their resistant subject populations. For example, the Egyptian pharaoh Thutmose III (reigned 1479–1425 B.C.E.) sought to eradicate the legitimacy of Queen Hatshepsut (reigned 1478–1458 B.C.E.), his predecessor and erstwhile co-ruler, by ordering widespread iconoclasm of her images. If destroying her many huge statues proved too big a task, the wreckers focused on her nose and eyes and inscriptions of her name.[15] Even more often, perhaps, concerns and struggles over doctrinal purity have prompted targeted iconoclasm. When Moses destroyed the golden calf Aaron had created for the Jews in his absence, the act was both an affirmation of his loyalty to the First and Second Commandments and an assertion of his rightful political leadership. Three thousand years later, the Protestant Reformation gained significant energies from well-orchestrated destruction of images of worship in Catholic churches.

In modern times, however, the destruction of cultural heritage appears to be more directly and massively associated with atrocities against minorities. Over the past several years, ISIS has frightened target populations into docility with attacks on their cultural heritage and leaders associated with it. Submission of local populations is often a desirable goal for a group that has sought to dominate occupied cities rather than simply scare their citizens away. While the targets of destruction may be closely aligned with Muslim sects that are abhorrent to ISIS ideology, such as Shi'a or Sufi Islam, they may also be objects or sites of ancient pre-Islamic worship that are not necessarily of great significance to contemporary populations but that have held various kinds of meaning as sources of tourist income or a general sense of belonging to an ancient land and culture. In ISIS ideology, a community's acquiescence to having such buildings or objects in their midst alone suffices to mark this heritage and its protectors for attack. The Islamic State's destruction of statues in the Mosul Museum in February 2015 and the wholesale destruction of the ancient temples of Baal Shamin and Bel in Palmyra later that year appear to have been designed to intimidate but also to convert new believers around the world to the Islamic State's cause. The bombings in Palmyra followed on the beheading of Khaled al-Asaad, the eighty-two-year-old supervising archaeologist for the site, an Alawite man who had refused to lead ISIS to the places where antiquities had been hidden.

Attacks on cultural heritage sites as tactics used to intimidate, subdue, or expel people are not one-sided in current conflicts in the Middle East. As part of its long campaign to expel rebel groups, the Syrian government perpetrated attacks on dense, historical inner cities and cultural sites. The regime appears to have targeted—or certainly not minded—religious and historic buildings of local significance, including the minaret and other major areas of the Sunni Mosque of Aleppo, whose roots lie in the Umayyad era. These attacks helped encourage minority populations to flee, propelling a form of "ethnic cleansing" that the government could then position as voluntary exile. The very targeting of a cultural monument can help pit ethnic and religious groups against each other to the advantage of a dominant power, even if neighboring communities may have had limited concerns about each other in the past.

If cultural sites, artifacts, and ritual traditions are among the most powerful forces that bond ethnic or national communities, their destruction may be seen as analogous to the process of depriving peoples of legal rights that often precedes attacks on their lives.[16] In the more recent cases of Syria and Iraq, attacks on mosques, shrines, and tombs are at the same time intended to strike down the people who visit those sites. In these situations religious and political grounds for cultural heritage destruction can be difficult to parse.

Humanists in the World

How can humanists possibly ameliorate the legal situations of refugees and immigrants who are unwanted by the governments or large population segments of their host countries? And if humanities scholars do not have the legal instruments to protect these applicant-citizens, how can they hope to protect their cultural heritage in war-torn countries? Sharply crafted op-eds citing Arendt or Giorgio Agamben have a role to play, but such interventions may not matter when both problems require the political and potentially military will of governments, and when for large swaths of citizens these groups are abstractions, easily demonized as alien, undesirable, or nonconforming.

Decades after World War II and a concatenation of genocides and conditions of prolonged statelessness for millions of displaced people, we can draw on so-called natural experiments to see what does and does not work. There are two major findings. First, internment camps creating false communities of the rightless, tolerated but given no chance at citizenship, breed hopelessness and resentment both in camps and in "host" countries, which treat the discontent of camp dwellers as a problem of policing.[17] Second, the most effective way to ameliorate the political condition of precarious immigrants is for them to make a visible economic contribution, sufficient for the host society to benefit but not so successful for the newcomers themselves to appear to threaten the prior citizenry of the receiving country. The political economist Peo Hansen has studied this dynamic: once Germany and Sweden had admitted large numbers of refugees in 2015, their governments had to relax the long-standing policy of fiscal austerity to be able to provide housing and services and to employ some of the asylum seekers. As Europe has negative population growth and need of skilled workers and an enhanced tax base to energize its sluggish economy, the investment has begun to pay off with new growth numbers in the communities where the refugees were concentrated. The

"refugee dividend" was so pronounced that a leading right-wing politician from the Sweden Democrats, an aggressive anti-immigration party,
asked for more refugees to be sent to his municipality of Boden.[18]

These two findings are coextensive: the most successful strategy for
supporting refugees, and one promoted actively by organizations such
as the International Rescue Committee and countries like Canada, is
resettlement in urban areas or other population centers where they can
be connected with local communities for health and social services, education, and potential employment and can contribute to the economy.
When people are seen to have families, even when those families may
look and sound radically alien to the local majority population, they have
a better chance of being accepted or at least tolerated. When members of
the family are known to be willing to work or provide services, such as
food stands, babysitting, or support in a local classroom or construction
site, a measure of normalcy may be established for the exiled, but also for
the community that has to figure out a stance toward them. If the services
and employment opportunities provided to refugees and immigrants of
uncertain status are also afforded in some measure to local citizens, resistance to the newcomers is mitigated.

In this sphere of civilian life, there is hope for the intervention of
humanists: of scholars and teachers who have made it their life's work to
understand the nuances of cultural expression and of difference, and of
what in culture unites people and what divides. The historian, the anthropologist, and the historian of art and literature have skills that can draw
out perspectives; prioritize what, in the massive archive of history and
culture, matters for questions that need to be asked today; represent those
findings through stories, documentary, and performance in a variety of
media and venues; and, perhaps most crucially, teach and help people
think with all this cultural material that presents us with difference as
well as convergence.

At least in Europe today, the encyclopedic museum is emerging as an
unexpected partner for the public humanities in the service of challenges
attendant on the arrival of new populations from distant lands. Paradoxically the Western museums that have long, and rightly, been seen as
complicit and self-interested in the denial of the rights of source communities to their cultural histories are now the guardians of the little
that is left once the instruments of contemporary warfare flatten historical districts, blow up ancient sites, and smash statues tagged as idols.

The encyclopedic museum of Enlightenment invention is a treasury of the great accomplishments of human cultures and individuals across time and geography, of the particularities of art and ritual that both unite and divide *Homo sapiens*. With its colonial histories of cultural control, extraction, and theft, that museum may be an unlikely generator of progressive intercultural action, having put many peoples at a permanent disadvantage in preserving, knowing, and enjoying their cultural histories. Nevertheless it is now often a best hope for connecting displaced peoples with the material and visual culture from which they have been divorced. Over the past couple of decades, Western museums have begun to come to terms with the responsibilities attached to what they acquired so often by acts of violence, asymmetrical power, and cultural erasure. Many are working with institutions and communities in countries of origin to lay a foundation for partial restitution and the sharing of histories. This work in progress, while far from finished and not always handled well, has given some museums the credibility to use their collections to engage with immigrant and refugee communities.

One of the most promising instances is the Multaqa project of the Berlin State Museums, the constellation of museums that is the encyclopedic repository of Prussian collections built from the Renaissance through the twenty-first century. As buildings, they project the same iconography of classical power as any other encyclopedic museum of colonial gestation, but as institutions they have come to rethink their relationships to peoples of the Middle East and elsewhere in more equitable terms. Multaqa, the Arabic word for "encounter" or "meeting point," was launched two years ago by the Museum for Islamic Art in consort with the Museum for Near Eastern Art and the Bode Museum of medieval and Renaissance sculpture and painting.[19] Stefan Weber, the director of the Museum for Islamic Art, worked in Syria for many years. In the summer of 2015, as Germany opened its borders to hundreds of thousands of refugees from Syria and Iraq, Weber reached out to a few recent arrivals he knew from his time in Syria and asked what he could do. An archaeologist told him he wanted the museum to put them to work. He made clear that most refugees were bored stiff in their resettlement flats, exhausted with the bureaucratic procedures, no matter how welcoming the country might be, and desperate to use their brains. Weber and his team went to the resettlement communities to invite applications for museum guide positions. The docents would be trained and paid to give tours of the museum's collection, in Arabic, for families, colleagues, and friends from their community. Within days the first twenty guides were hired, and the museum began to learn their stories and provide them with accelerated German-language training. The initial sessions were held in the Near Eastern section of the Pergamon Museum. When you come into that museum, the first thing you see is the Ishtar Gate built in Babylon in the sixth century B.C.E. As the refugees gathered for their first meeting, an Iraqi participant asked, "Why is this gate here?" His opening gambit led to sustained conversations and disagreements among the group that are replayed to this day in the interactive tours led by the docents. Is the story of the acquisition not another example of how the West has always been selfish in relation to the refugees' region of origin? Most Iraqis and some Syrians agree, but other Iraqis say that given the state of things in their country, it may be a good thing that this great monument has been preserved in Berlin. Others marvel that Germany would build a magnificent edifice just to fit this and other huge structures from back home that, come to think of it, they had not thought about too much. Some get angry and are not convinced, noting that Western engagements in the region have created all that instability and held the countries back from developing their own capacities to take care of these great things. Others relish the recognition of domestic and religious objects redolent of a lost home. Through all these conversations, the program has been as eye-opening to museum staff as it has been engaging for the refugees.

Weber put two recent Syrian arrivals in charge of the program; one is now pursuing a Ph.D. in archaeology, and the other, who had started law school in Syria, wants to become a human rights lawyer. Professors from the Free University of Berlin, who had already been working with the museum on narratives around the complex intercultural histories of objects in the museum, helped inform the program. The two leaders from Syria worked with museum colleagues to start a word-of-mouth and social media campaign about the tours to come, and also crafted more extended workshops on topics of interest to their community. Almost ten thousand visitors have been served. The program has been so successful that many German citizens have asked for the tours in German so that they can engage with the refugee community, and the museums are exploring that possibility.

As more people came and more guides were hired, tours of different museums were added. Women seemed drawn especially to tours at the

Bode Museum, where most of the art represents Christian themes. These tours laid bare the complex religious and ethnic makeup of the refugee community. Some Muslim guests were unimpressed by the incessant representation of holy figures of Islam such as Mary, Joseph, and Jesus, while members of the Christian Syriac and Roman Catholic communities felt the city finally had something to offer. Whatever their views, these groups found that the objects gave them an opportunity to talk about religion and to realize that before 2011 they had rarely worried so incessantly over who was Christian, Druze, Alawite, or Sunni.

Other museums wanted in. The Multaqa team asked the community what interested them. The prevailing response was the history of the country that had welcomed them in. A year and a half later, tours and discussion programs in the German Historical Museum are requested most by docents as well as visitors. Some report taking comfort in the idea that Germany could have recovered from a disastrous history of aggressive war and genocide of ethnic minorities to become a vibrant democracy that is helping refugees overcome trauma of somewhat similar origins. The guides are so articulate about what their work means to them that I have to quote one of them, Bashar Almahfoud, a mechanical engineer from Syria who is talking about the film footage he shows of a bombed-out Nuremberg and Dresden:

> When the visitors realize the difference between Germany then and how it looks today, they have hopes that their own country could be rebuilt some day. That encourages many of them, and many come to the museum tours again to learn more. I myself am especially enthusiastic about the enormous achievement and strength of will of the women who rebuilt after 1945. I convey that to my visitors. In the section on the Industrial Revolution at the beginning of the twentieth century, I have already spoken about the growing role of women in the society and how they successfully struggled for their rights. This is very important to me, in order to underscore the equality of women and men, which everyone who wants to live in Germany must understand and acknowledge.[20]

The project has had two effects that expand its meaning beyond the people who are reached directly. First, the Museum for Islamic Art has built such extensive networks with the community that they have been able to step up a major effort to involve Syrians, both refugees and those still in the country, in gathering material for the Syrian Heritage Archive Project. This initiative collects, documents, and makes available online testimonies, maps, photographs, videos, and stories about places where destruction of the built environment and social fabric has been most severe. Second, the project has been a source of pride for many in Germany—possibly a helpful fact for a government that put its thumb on the scale of asylum when most Western countries balked.[21]

As the Multaqa project shows, the Western museum has a fighting chance to turn a history of exploitative collecting into engagement with and genuine support for communities that have a stake in their holdings. The potential of the public humanities to create channels through which formal institutions and constituencies that have diffuse but real stakes in them benefit from and contribute to each other's enlightenment and capacities for empathy is strikingly clear here. The humanities disciplines that nourished the museum—art history, anthropology, classics, and conservation—need to be present in this process, not least because their disciplines were complicit with archaeologists digging up treasure or curators going on collecting missions without much regard for communities of origin. If these disciplines can help make the museum a true community resource and a place for difficult conversations, they can model mindful public behavior for other disciplines and their cultural heritage institutions.

In the United States the humanities are being deployed inventively to address questions of immigration that are putting the democratic intuition and its institutions under great strain.[22] The New York Historical Society offers free courses based in its collections to help immigrants prepare for the citizenship exam; other humanities institutions, such as the Worcester Art Museum, have begun to make their sites available for citizenship swearing-in ceremonies. Such activities can also come from within the academy and radiate outward. In 2009 Jason de León, then a newly minted anthropologist, felt discomfort at the prospect of continuing his traditional archaeological research on Olmec culture. While working on his dissertation, he had met many Mexican people whose families had sought to cross the border to the U.S. illegally or who had been unsuccessful. A colleague working in the Sonora Desert of Arizona mentioned that from time to time she found evidence left behind by migrants striving to cross the border, from empty water bottles and tattered backpacks to worn-out children's shoes and even a love letter. Asking himself what an archaeology of undocumented migration in the Southwest might be, De León launched the Undocumented Migration Project, an effort to locate, retrieve, document, and analyze what people leave behind on their treacherous journeys.

With the involvement of many students, the project has retrieved and documented ten thousand objects, produced several exhibitions, and yielded a major study by De León, *The Land of Open Graves: Living and Dying on the Migrant Trail* (2015). It became a source for an innovative virtual reality installation by the filmmaker Alejandro González Iñárritu, called *Carne y Arena* (Flesh and Sand), which confronts visitors with the dangers of the desert-crossing experience and puts names and faces to migrants who have tried.

The project is no mere exercise in curiosity. Interviewing migrants and border control personnel, investigating human remains and the changing character of objects found in the desert, De León unearthed a national security paradigm that is little known. Because border cities like El Paso and San Diego are heavily policed, migrants are forced to try their luck in remote areas like the Arizona desert, where the unforgiving terrain may deter or mete out "natural" punishment, and the unwanted migrant crisis stays out of public view. In De León's successful tenure process at the University of Michigan, the question arose whether he was a proper archaeologist or an anthropologist. What is without doubt is the courage it must have taken for him to stake his academic career on a redeployment of his investigative and storytelling skills to make visible the violence that our legal and policing protocols inflict on the most vulnerable people fleeing insecurity.

In Europe and in America, in South Africa and India, in South Korea and Australia, in Brazil and Mexico, the humanities community has countless opportunities to teach to the question of how we interact with newcomers when they are numerous and, as Arendt put it, already branded by regimes of origin or destination as "scum of the earth." Humanists have at their disposal the resources of political philosophy and ethnographic inquiry, traditions of writing and public engagement, collections of libraries, archives, and museums, and the communicative potentials of the arts to put the humanities to work in the world and to prepare their students to do so. The humanities can credibly draw on the reservoirs of thought and method they have built over many centuries and refresh them through their socialization of new groups of students who enter the academy from the world every year. Those students are changing, but their demands for engagement and relevance will not go away. Questions of who belongs in the polity, and how, can be opened up by interacting with people whose lives are precarious and whose very cultural heritage is often the humanist object of study. I hope that these few examples among many have suggested that if the humanities bring their analytical and expressive capabilities to research and teaching with these fundamentally humanistic problems, they manifest their relevance and may lay claim to resources that often seem in such short supply.

Notes

1. For the Mellon Foundation's mission and programs, see https://mellon.org. I have the privilege of overseeing the Foundation's grantmaking and research programs. I am grateful to Hent de Vries, director of the School of Criticism and Theory, for inviting me to present these thoughts at the School's 2017 summer session at Cornell University, and for his and the audience's stimulating comments. Elements of the paper were also presented and discussed at the World Humanities Conference in Liège and at the annual conference of the Consortium of Humanities Centers and Institutes in Cape Town, both in August 2017. Thanks also to Alberta Arthurs, Ignacio López-Calvo, and James Shulman for their close readings and thoughtful suggestions.

2. Harpham, "Beneath and Beyond," argues that the notion of "crisis" is historically closely associated with the definition of the humanities in their own right and offers powerful arguments against doomsday thinking about their future.

3. American Academy of Arts and Sciences, *Humanities Indicators*. The *Humanities Indicators* are partly funded by the Mellon Foundation.

4. As figure 2 shows, humanities undergraduate degrees as a percentage of all degrees reached its highest point in history around 1967, when it stood at 17 percent. The *Humanities Indicators* data for current humanities disciplines go back to 1987, when that percentage was about 12 percent.

5. Schmidt, "Gender and the Long-Term Decline"; Tworek, "The Real Reason."

6. At public universities in states that have strong articulation agreements for student transfer, large numbers of humanities majors are transfer students from community colleges. At the University of California, Los Angeles, for example, 47 percent of humanities majors have transferred from two-year colleges (communication from David Schaberg, dean of humanities at UCLA, October 2015); at the University of Washington, 50 percent of humanities majors have come from two-year colleges according to Simpson Center for the Humanities, "Reimagining the Humanities Ph.D."

7. Woodward, "We Are All," has made a powerful case for rethinking how we describe, teach, and study the humanities, with an emphasis on their reform in public higher education.

8. Said, *The World*, esp. 1–53.

9. Arendt, *The Origins*, ix.

10. Ibid., 295–96. Giorgio Agamben in *Homo Sacer* has further analyzed the paradoxes and vulnerabilities of this condition of "bare life," of merely being a biological human, that arises as soon as a human body loses political rights.

11. Article 1 of the 1951 Refugee Convention, as amended by the 1967 Protocol, defines a refugee as "a person who owing to a well-founded fear of being persecuted for reasons of race, religion, nationality, membership of a particular social group or political opinion, is outside the country of his nationality and is unable or, owing to such fear, is unwilling to avail himself of the protection of that country; or who, not having a nationality and being outside the country of his former habitual residence as a result of such events, is unable or, owing to such fear, is unwilling to return to it." The insufficiency of international legal protocols for refugees, which were born of the sovereign nation-state system that forms the basis for the United Nations and offices such as the United Nations High Commissioner for Refugees, has been forcefully critiqued by Alexander Betts and Paul Collier in *Refuge*, 41–43 and passim.

12. Arendt saw how the dynamic of post–World War I denationalization of minorities produced this paradoxical tautology: "Those whom the persecutor had singled out as scum of the earth—Jews, Trotskyites, etc.—actually were received as scum of the earth everywhere; those whom persecution had called undesirable became the *indésirables* of Europe. The official SS newspaper, the *Schwarze Korps*, stated explicitly in 1938 that if the world was not yet convinced that the Jews were the scum of the earth, it soon would be when unidentifiable beggars, without nationality, without money, and without passports crossed their frontiers" (*Origins*, 269).

13. Ibid., 296. Earlier in the text, Arendt has already noted the oddity that the criminal has more rights than the stateless: "The best criterion by which to decide whether someone has been forced outside the pale of the law is to ask if he would benefit by committing a crime. If a small burglary is likely to improve his legal position, at least temporarily, one may be sure that he has been deprived of human rights. For then a criminal offense becomes the best opportunity to regain some kind of human equality, even if it be as a recognized exception to the norm. The one important fact is that this exception is provided for by law. As a criminal even a stateless person will not be treated worse than another criminal, that is, he will be treated like everybody else. Only as an offender of the law can he gain protection from it" (286).

14. For a trenchant analysis of "the new warfare," a term coined by Christine Chinkin and Mary Kaldor, see their *International Law and New Wars*. Chinkin and Kaldor briefly note that cultural heritage destruction is one weapon in a much broader arsenal of tactics of war in the long-term, multiparty, diffuse, and

intractable local conflicts that have arisen since the dissolution of the Soviet Union and the end of Cold War polarization. My thinking about the connections between cultural heritage destruction and the plight of displaced persons is indebted to the conference Responsibility to Protect Cultural Heritage organized by the American Academy of Arts and Sciences and the Getty Trust, held at the British Academy in December 2016, where Mary Kaldor elaborated further on new warfare tactics.

15. As a minor, Thutmose III had notionally reigned jointly with his step-mother, Hatshepsut, an extremely successful pharaoh, for nineteen years until her death. Iconoclasm against rivals was not unprecedented in ancient Egypt; in Hatshepsut's case, her gender may have constituted a particular challenge for Thutmose III and his heir, Amenhotep II, as it contravened a millennium and a half of mostly male Egyptian kingship. Roehrig et al., *Hatshepsut*.

16. Arendt, *Origins*, esp. 267–90.

17. Betts and Collier, *Refuge*, esp. 52–55, 77–78, 136–40.

18. Hansen, "Asylum *or* Austerity?"

19. See Museum für Islamische Kunst, "Multaqa"; *Universes in Universe*, "Multaka's Favorites."

20. See Museum für Islamische Kunst, "Multaqa"; *Universes in Universe*, "Multaka's Favorites."

21. In 2016 the program won Germany's Special Award for Projects Promoting Cultural Integration of Refugees, and came in first in the annual competition Landmarks in the Land of Ideas in the Culture category, among other distinctions.

22. For the concept of "democratic intuition," see Spivak, "What Is It to Vote?"

Works Cited

Agamben, Giorgio. *Homo Sacer: Sovereign Power and Bare Life*. Translated by Daniel Heller-Roazen. Stanford, Calif.: Stanford University Press, 1998.

American Academy of Arts and Sciences. *Humanities Indicators*. Accessed August 17, 2017. https://www.humanitiesindicators.org/default.aspx.

Arendt, Hannah. *The Origins of Totalitarianism*. New York: Schocken Books, 1951.

Betts, Alexander, and Paul Collier. *Refuge: Transforming a Broken Refugee System*. London: Allen Lane, 2017.

Chinkin, Christine, and Mary Kaldor. *International Law and New Wars*. Cambridge, U.K.: Cambridge University Press, 2017.

De León, Jason. *The Land of Open Graves: Living and Dying on the Migrant Trail*. Oakland: University of California Press, 2015.

Hansen, Peo. "Asylum *or* Austerity? The 'Refugee Crisis' and the Keynesian Interlude." *European Political Science* 17, no. 1 (2017): 128–39. https://doi.org/10.1057/s41304-017-0122-y.

Harpham, Geoffrey. "Beneath and Beyond the 'Crisis in the Humanities.'" *New Literary History* 36, no. 1 (2005): 21–36.

Museum für Islamische Kunst. "Multaqa: Museum as Meeting Point—Refugees as Guides in Berlin Museums." Accessed October 10, 2017. http://www.smb .museum/en/museums-institutions/museum-fuer-islamische-kunst/collection -research/research-cooperation/multaka.html.

Roehrig, Catherine, et al. *Hatshepsut: From Queen to Pharaoh.* Exhibition catalogue. New York: Metropolitan Museum of Art, 2005.

Said, Edward W. *The World, the Text, and the Critic.* Cambridge, Mass.: Harvard University Press, 1983.

Schmidt, Ben. "Gender and the Long-Term Decline in Humanities Enrollments." *Sapping Attention,* June 26, 2013. http://sappingattention.blogspot.com/2013 /06/gender-and-long-term-decline-in.html.

Simpson Center for the Humanities. "Reimagining the Humanities Ph.D. and Reaching New Publics." Accessed October 10, 2017. https://simpsoncenter.org /programs/public-scholarship/reimagining-humanities-phd-and-reaching-new -publics.

Spivak, Gayatri Chakravorty. "What Is It to Vote?" In *Gendered Citizenship and the Politics of Representation: Citizenship, Gender and Diversity,* edited by H. Danielsen et al., 17–36. London: Palgrave, 2016.

Tworek, Heidi. "The Real Reason the Humanities Are 'in Crisis.'" *The Atlantic.* December 18, 2013. https://www.theatlantic.com/education/archive/2013/12 /the-real-reason-the-humanities-are-in-crisis/282441/.

Universes in Universe. "Bashar Almahfoud: War-Damaged German Cities." Accessed September 12, 2017. https://universes.art/specials/multaka-berlin /bashar-almahfoud/.

———. "Multaka's Favorites in 4 Berlin Museums." Accessed September 12, 2017. https://universes.art/specials/multaka-berlin/.

Woodward, Kathleen. "We Are All Nontraditional Learners Now: Community Colleges, Long-Life Learning, and Problem-Solving Humanities." In *A New Deal for the Humanities: Liberal Arts and the Future of Higher Education,* edited by Gordon Hunter and Feisal G. Mohamed, 51–71. New Brunswick, N.J.: Rutgers University Press, 2016.

Keywords: A Refresher on Humanism and Praxis

Doris Sommer

An accelerated rhythm of social, economic, political, and personal change in this new century obliges us to innovate just in order to understand the dynamics, let alone to participate in productive and ethical ways. And the politically chilling effects of clogged and abandoned democratic practices make the challenge ever more urgent. How does one think innovatively when existing concepts describe existing forms and activities rather than new possibilities? And alternatively, how does one refresh practices when innovative thinking seems blocked? Why have useful words like "praxis" faded into disuse, as if intellectuals had no recourse but to imagine that theory and intervention were unrelated activities? This disconnect amounts to confirming our isolationist bubble as a privileged sanctuary amid a broad and increasingly frustrated general public. Part of a civically responsible answer to the blockage and blockade is to engage intellectual creativity in the service of generating new concepts and refreshing forgotten tools to name novel ideas and perceptions.

Humanism today needs to recover its inaugural and long-standing civic mission. That mission to establish collaborations between reason and judgment motivated Immanuel Kant to celebrate art as the medium of communication for ideas and feelings that are so new and still formless that they don't yet have names. Raymond Williams offered a version of this Kantian appreciation for art's capacity to generate concepts. He called it "structure of feeling," a neologism that captures the preconceptual period where new ideas still gestate, before they are christened.

Therefore, among the works created by artistic experimentation are words that describe art's accomplishments. The circularity is inevitable. Naming both follows from and fosters the recognition of novelty. For example, before the production of a "baroque" style, the word meant something else; the same is true of "montage," while "melodrama" is a new name for a new genre. Words get recruited retrospectively, once a structure of feeling achieves conceptual clarity, to publicly legitimate an addition to our consciousness. It is the public use of words that promotes enlightened freethinking, Kant insisted; private pleasures and rationality cannot amount to world-making.[1]

As humanists who may share a sensation that universities have been generators of pessimism over the past two or three generations, this reflection on neologisms should come as a relief. There is no need to insist on using tired words while trying to communicate complex new formations. The words are often pathological—"poverty," "corruption," "inequality"—and they dominate in literary criticism, sociology, history, aesthetics, politics, economics, and so on. Instead of tangling with conventional themes of almost paralyzing weight, we would do well to access underemployed keywords as entry points into intersecting fields of the humanities and social sciences in order to locate points of dynamism. Particular words and new uses represent advances in scholarship because they are forged to signal a novel idea or ways of thinking. This means that the surest way to get into theoretical material isn't to tease out an argument but simply to identify its peculiar vocabulary. We can cut straight to the lexicon, not by taking a shortcut or jaywalking but rather by acknowledging the flashing lights that signal theory's efficient distillation of complex processes.

Mentioning keywords is a grateful nod to Williams, whose *Keywords* (1976) is a reference for all our related disciplines in the "human sciences." Williams wrote the book because he did not understand what everyday words meant after World War II. Profound changes in society, politics, economics, and personhood made him trace changes in everyday unexamined uses of language. The most troubling word for Williams was "culture." And thanks to his reflection on that fundamental word, we can acknowledge that the trouble comes from the fact that "culture" has two rather distinct and disconnected meanings, though users employ the word as if one or the other were the obvious meaning, that is, without acknowledging the difference that disables communication. This blind spot or fault line along cultural lines has been blocking our best efforts toward development, on both sides of the divide.

On the one hand, for social sciences, culture means a heritage of shared beliefs and practices. Consider Max Weber's foundational book, *The Protestant Ethic and the Spirit of Capitalism* (1905), as exemplary for the fields of sociology, economics, anthropology, and even history. A defining feature for capitalism, in Weber's book, as the culture that derived from the Protestant ethic, is to wage a "war on pleasure." Weber warned that this unfeeling rationality would generate an "iron cage" to trap our humanity. But his book has been read, paradoxically, as a manual for the lockdown. On the other hand, for artists and humanists, culture feeds on pleasure and produces more. It describes a field of artistic experiment, trial and error, along with practically infinite interpretations fueled by the energies of wonder and doubt.

All the while that one definition of culture remains deaf to the other, we cannot offer significant or lasting change. If decision makers schooled in the social sciences continue to see culture as a mere backdrop or an obstacle for policy, and if artists continue to produce alleged interventions that ignore existing practices in a spirit of unbounded freedom, we will stay stuck in the fault line and shirk a responsibility that W. E. B. Du Bois assigned: "to be a co-worker in the kingdom of culture."[2] Real change is the product of a dynamic set in motion when clever interventions interrupt established paradigms and co-construct alternative arrangements.

Responding to Weber's dour sociological predictions, we can enlist the optimism of the humanist Antonio Gramsci to suggest how culture can spike development. For Gramsci, the precondition for transformational social change was the broad engagement of masses as empowered collectives (Weber dangerously favored charismatic leaders), and pleasure in idiosyncratic forms of artistic as well as rooted expression was the fuel for participating in personal and shared advances. This pleasure in art and collective interpretation contrasts with the exclusionary rituals of commodified pleasure typical of capitalist consumerism. Gramsci's confidence in the transformational role of creative culture provides a framework for understanding a new wave of inclusive artistic practices that can revive the arts as vehicles for active citizenship. Participatory art has the potential to re-enchant today's sorely disenchanted sociocultural world of mature capitalism.

The conceptual debt to Williams is obvious here. Without a lexical recalibration regarding culture in order to resignify misunderstanding as opportunities for collaboration, engagement and praxis will fail. But in formal terms, the remaining contribution of this invitation to rethink the humanities is in primary debt to another intimate ally. I mean Roland Barthes. Like Williams, Barthes performs the leveling and mutual visibility of concepts by demoting them all to an arbitrary arrangement of alphabetical order. But his gesture of raising the invisible to visibility takes an added risk. Barthes writes of love. His glossary of love puts vulnerability and interpersonal risk in public view.

Just as Barthes affirmed love's ubiquity despite its erasure from public speech, engaged humanists or cultural agents note that talking about ever-present art in its civic and practical functions has been relegated beyond recognized academic disciplines. This institutional indifference to social and everyday arts is the impoverishment that John Dewey decried in *Art as Experience* (1933). He claimed that decontextualized "art works" were imprisoned in museums and galleries. Art is practical for Dewey, and one recognizes art in the experience of incitement to action, of being shaken and moved to produce more works. He celebrated creative practices in everyday life and venerated the innate human capacity for innovation. We co-create the changing world thanks to an irrepressible instinct to play, a psychological drive that Friedrich Schiller coined in 1794 the *Spieltrieb*.[3] Schiller's lesson includes a lead to coin new words. We will need them to refresh a field of engaged humanities.

Appendix

acupuncture: micro urban/cultural interventions with macro effects; Jaime Lerner, Antanas Mockus

admiration: basic sentiment of citizenship, stronger than tolerance; Antanas Mockus

aesthetics: intersubjective reflection on the impact of beauty or the sublime; Immanuel Kant

allegory: dialectical toggle between history and nature, making and finding; Walter Benjamin

amphibian: translator, communicator, from one cultural register to another; Antanas Mockus

art: artifice, device, to make comprehension difficult and refresh perception; Viktor Shklovsky

artist: a nonvictim, someone who is free to make soft constraints and to experiment

beauty: that which pleases without interests or concepts; Immanuel Kant

catharsis: purge rebelliousness, Aristotle; banish the cop in the head, Augusto Boal

civic culture: articulation of law, morality, popular culture; Antanas Mockus

color: structural element in the Renaissance of Tirana, Albania; Edi Rama

common sense: intersubjective agreement after aesthetic judgment; Immanuel Kant

connectionist: agent who fosters collaborations; Pedro Reyes

constraints: hard and soft, imposed and also chosen conditions of rational choice; Jon Elster

culture 1: social sciences heritage of beliefs and practices

culture 2: arts and humanities field for experiments, paradigm shifts, exploration

distribution of the sensible: range of access to and production of art; Jacques Rancière

empathy: temptation to replace another's feelings or to be replaced; Augusto Boal

estrangement: effect of making the familiar strange, surprising; Viktor Shklovsky

ethics: first philosophy; Emmanuel Lévinas

experience: generative excitement ignited by art; John Dewey

facilitator: multiplier of a creative practice; Augusto Boal

forum theater: interactive improvisation to explore options beyond tragedy; Augusto Boal

habitualization: boredom through familiar anticipation, indifference; Viktor Shklovsky

harmonize: neutralize dissent, Jacques Rancière; repair rift of culture, law, morality, Antanas Mockus

hegemony: unspoken contract between unequal partners; Antonio Gramsci

humanities: the only academic field that enjoys doubt

hybrid: toggling between traditional and modern forms; Néstor García Canclini

ignorant schoolmaster: facilitator, as opposed to explicator; Jacques Rancière

infinity: atemporal and unknowable otherness; Emmanuel Lévinas

judgment: innate faculty of sociability developed through aesthetics; Immanuel Kant

listener: partner who guides the narrative; Italo Calvino

love: Roland Barthes, Paulo Freire, Martha Nussbaum

performance: consciousness of artifice in acting; Augusto Boal, Diana Taylor

pleasure: a shared feeling that promotes positive social change; Antanas Mockus

praxis: refinement of theory and intervention when contradictions become horizons; Antonio Gramsci

pre-texts: teacher-training as facilitator for artistic interpretations of classic texts

projection: casting arresting images onto public buildings and monuments, e.g., Krzysztof Wodiczko

reader: profession supported by tobacco rollers in the Spanish Caribbean, Havana, Tampa, NYC, etc.

recycle: basic operation of all arts, including the network of Cartonera publishers

responsibility: my nonreciprocal obligation to the other; Emmanuel Lévinas

saying: the act of communication, as distinct from the message; Edward Said; Emmanuel Lévinas

secrets: claim of privileged information to affirm authority; Rigoberta Menchú

silence: indicator of fundamental shared ideas and values; Pierre Macherey

slaps and embraces: syncopated approach to seduce powerful partner; Toni Morrison

spect-actor: any participant from audience can intervene on stage; Augusto Boal

Spieltrieb: play drive fueled by the conflict between reason and sensuality; Friedrich Schiller

squares and rectangles: indigenous weaves convertible to couture curves; Carla Fernández

sub-art: creative social practice without the pretension of disinterestedness; Antanas Mockus

sublime: aesthetic effect ignited by horror or fear after being processed by reason; Immanuel Kant

surprise: the basic effect of art, initial lack of understanding that prompts curiosity

sympathy: sentiment that fosters solidarity; Augusto Boal

tragedy: the failure of imagination, assumption of nothing to be done; Augusto Boal

transactional: the reciprocal dynamic of learning and teaching; John Dewey, Paulo Freire

war of position: staggered revolution through cultural change; Antonio Gramsci

wedge: weakness of rigid structure as entry point to make change; Paulo Freire

wit: the effect of semiotic condensation and/or displacement; Sigmund Freud

Notes

1. Kant, "What Is Enlightenment?"
2. Du Bois, *Souls of Black Folk*, 3.
3. Schiller, *Literary and Philosophical Essays*, 211–313.

Works Cited

Dewey, John. *Art as Experience*. 1933. New York: Perigee Books, 2005.

Du Bois, W. E. B. *Souls of Black Folk*. Oxford: Oxford University Press, 2007.

Kant, Immanuel. "What Is Enlightenment?" In *Practical Philosophy*. Translated and edited by Mary J. Gregor. Cambridge, U.K.: Cambridge University Press, 1996.

Schiller, Friedrich. *Literary and Philosophical Essays: French, German and Italian. Vol. 32: Letters on the Aesthetic Education of Man*. Harvard Classics. New York: P. F. Collier and Son, 1910.

Weber, Max. *The Protestant Ethic and the Spirit of Capitalism: And Other Writings*. New York: Penguin, 2002.

Williams, Raymond. *Keywords*. Oxford: Oxford University Press, 2014.

CONTRIBUTORS

K. Anthony Appiah is a professor of philosophy and law at NYU. He was born in London (where his Ghanaian father was a law student) but moved as an infant to Kumasi, Ghana, where he grew up. His father, Joseph Emmanuel Appiah, a lawyer and politician, was also, at various times, a member of Parliament, an ambassador, and president of the Ghana Bar Association; his English mother, the novelist and children's writer Peggy Appiah, was active in the social, philanthropic, and cultural life of Kumasi. Appiah took B.A. and Ph.D. degrees in philosophy at Cambridge University and has taught philosophy in Ghana, France, Britain, and the United States. He explored questions of African and African American identity in his book *In My Father's House: Africa in the Philosophy of Culture* (1992); examined the cultural dimensions of global citizenship in *Cosmopolitanism: Ethics in a World of Strangers* (2006); and investigated the social and individual importance of identity in *The Ethics of Identity* (2005). In 2012 he received the National Humanities Medal from President Barack Obama. His latest book, from Harvard University Press, is *As If: Idealizations and Ideals*.

David Castillo is the University at Buffalo director of the Humanities Institute and a professor of Spanish in the Department of Romance Languages and Literatures, where he served as chair between 2009 and 2015. He is the author of *Awry Views: Anamorphosis, Cervantes, and the Early Picaresque* (2001) and *Baroque Horrors: Roots of the Fantastic in the Age of Curiosities* (2010; paperback 2012) and coauthor of *Zombie Talk: Culture, History, Politics* (2016) and *Medialogies: Reading Reality in the Age of Inflationary Media* (2016). Castillo has also coedited *Reason and Its Others: Italy, Spain, and the New World* (2006), *Spectacle and Topophilia: Reading Early and Postmodern Hispanic Cultures* (2012), and *Writing in the End Times: Apocalyptic Imagination in the Hispanic World* (2018).

William Egginton is the Decker Professor in the Humanities and director of the Alexander Grass Humanities Institute at Johns Hopkins University. His research and teaching focus on Spanish and Latin American literature, literary theory, and the relation between literature and philosophy. He is the author of numerous books, including *How the World Became a Stage* (2003), *Perversity and Ethics* (2006), *A Wrinkle in History* (2007), *The Philosopher's Desire* (2007), *The Theater of Truth* (2010), *In Defense of Religious Moderation* (2011), *The Man Who Invented Fiction: How Cervantes Ushered in the Modern World* (2016), and, with David Castillo, *Medialogies: Reading Reality in the Age of Inflationary Media* (2017). He is also the coeditor, with Mike Sandbothe, of *The Pragmatic*

Turn in Philosophy (2004) and, with David E. Johnson, of *Thinking with Borges* (2009), as well as the translator of Lisa Block de Behar's *Borges, the Passion of an Endless Quotation* (2003). His most recent book is *The Splintering of the American Mind* (2018).

David Theo Goldberg is the director of the University of California Humanities Research Institute, the University of California's system-wide research facility for the human sciences and theoretical research in the arts. He also holds faculty appointments as a professor of comparative literature, anthropology, and criminology, law and society at UC Irvine. Goldberg's work ranges over issues of political theory, race and racism, critical theory, cultural studies, digital humanities, and humanities and the future of the university. He was the principal cofounder of HASTAC, the Humanities, Arts, Social Science Advanced Collaborator, to promote partnerships among the human sciences, arts, social sciences, and technology and supercomputing interests for advancing research, teaching, and public outreach. He has authored numerous books, including *Are We All Postracial Yet?* (2015), *Sites of Race* (2014), *The Future of Thinking* (2009), *The Racial State* (2002), *Racial Subjects: Race and Writing in America* (1997), *Racist Culture: Philosophy and the Politics of Meaning* (1993), and *Ethical Theory: Texts and Contexts* (1989). He has also edited or coedited many volumes. Earlier in his career Goldberg produced independent films and music videos (some of which aired on MTV) and codirected the award-winning short film on South Africa, *The Is/land.*

Ignacio López-Calvo is a professor of Latin American literature at the University of California, Merced. He is the author of more than seventy articles and book chapters, as well as eight books on Latin American and U.S. Latino literature and culture: *Saudades of Japan and Brazil: Contested Modernities in Lusophone Nikkei Cultural Production* (forthcoming), *Dragons in the Land of the Condor: Tusán Literature and Knowledge in Peru* (2014), *The Affinity of the Eye: Writing Nikkei in Peru* (2013), *Latino Los Angeles in Film and Fiction: The Cultural Production of Social Anxiety* (2011), *Imaging the Chinese in Cuban Literature and Culture* (2007), *"Trujillo and God": Literary and Cultural Representations of the Dominican Dictator* (2005), *Religión y militarismo en la obra de Marcos Aguinis 1963–2000* (2002), and *Written in Exile: Chilean Fiction from 1973–Present* (2001). He has also edited the books *Latinx Writing Los Angeles: Nonfiction Dispatches from a Decolonial Rebellion* (forthcoming), *The Humanities in a World Upside Down* (2017), *Contemporary Latin American Fiction* (2017), *Critical Insights: Roberto Bolaño* (2015), *Roberto Bolaño, a Less Distant Star: Critical Essays* (2015), *Magical Realism (Critical Insights)* (2014), *Peripheral Transmodernities: South-to-South Dialogues between the Luso-Hispanic World and "the Orient"* (2012), *Alternative Orientalisms in Latin America and Beyond* (2007), and *One World Periphery Reads the Other: Knowing the "Oriental" in the Americas and the Iberian Peninsula* (2009), and he coedited *Caminos para* *la paz: Literatura israelí y árabe en castellano* (2008). He is the co-executive director of the academic journal *Transmodernity: Journal of Peripheral Cultural Production of the Luso-Hispanic World*, the co-executive director of the Palgrave Macmillan book series Historical and Cultural Interconnections between Latin America and Asia, and the executive director of the Anthem Press book series Anthem Studies in Latin American Literature and Culture.

Christina Lux is the associate director of the Center for the Humanities at UC Merced. Her work has appeared in the *Journal of Transnational American Studies*, the *International Journal of Francophone Studies*, and *Metamorphoses: A Journal of Literary Translation*. Her poetry has appeared on National Public Radio, in the *Houston Chronicle*, and in journals such as *Women's Studies Quarterly*, *North Dakota Quarterly*, the *Delmarva Review*, *Feminist Formations*, *Salome Magazine*, and *27 rue de fleures*, as well as in books from Oxford University Press and Woodley Press, among other presses. She holds a Ph.D. in Romance Languages from the University of Oregon.

Robert D. Newman is the president and director of the National Humanities Center. He has published six books: *Transgressions of Reading: Narrative Engagement as Exile and Return* (1993), *Centuries Ends, Narrative Means* (editor, 1996), *Pedagogy, Praxis, Ulysses: Using Joyce's Text to Transform the Classroom* (editor, 1996), *Joyce's Ulysses: The Larger Perspective* (coeditor, 1987), *Understanding Thomas Pynchon* (1986), *Uncommon Threads: Reading and Writing about Contemporary America* (coauthor, 2003), in addition to numerous articles and reviews on modern and contemporary literature and culture as well as several poems. For the past eighteen years, he has also been the general editor for the Cultural Frames, Framing Culture series published by University of Virginia Press. Much of his current work focuses on public advocacy for the humanities.

David Palumbo-Liu is the Louise Hewlett Nixon Professor and a professor of comparative literature and, by courtesy, of English, at Stanford University. He is the author most recently of *The Deliverance of Others: Reading Literature in a Global Age* (2012) and the coeditor of *Immanuel Wallerstein and the Problem of the World: System, Scale, Culture* (2011). He is the founding editor of *Occasion: Interdisciplinary Studies in the Humanities* (http://arcade.stanford.edu/occasion-issues) and founded and directs the TeachingHumanRights.org collaboratory. His blogs have appeared in *The Nation*, *Salon*, *The Guardian*, *Truthout*, *Al Jazeera*, *AlterNet*, and other venues; he is a contributing editor for the *Los Angeles Review of Books*. He is on the Executive Council of the Modern Language Association and is the vice president of the American Comparative Literature Association; he will assume the presidency in 2019.

Doris Sommer is the director of the Cultural Agents Initiative at Harvard University and the Ira and Jewell Williams Professor of Romance Languages and

Literatures and of African and African American Studies. Her academic and outreach work promotes development through arts and humanities, specifically through Pre-Texts in Boston Public Schools, throughout Latin America, and beyond. Pre-Texts is an arts-based training program for teachers of literacy, critical thinking, and citizenship. Among her books are *Foundational Fictions: The National Romances of Latin America* (1991), about novels that helped to consolidate new republics; *Proceed with Caution When Engaged by Minority Literature* (1999), on a rhetoric of particularism; *Bilingual Aesthetics: A New Sentimental Education* (2004); and *The Work of Art in the World: Civic Agency and Public Humanities* (2014). Sommer has enjoyed and is dedicated to developing good public school education. She has a B.A. from New Jersey's Douglass College for Women and a Ph.D. from Rutgers University.

Mariët Westermann is the executive vice president of the Andrew W. Mellon Foundation, where she oversees the grantmaking and research programs and has created initiatives in graduate education reform, partnerships between community colleges and research universities, research on the value of liberal arts education, support for refugee scholars and artists, and arts and cultural heritage preservation. Westermann was the first provost of New York University Abu Dhabi, charged with developing the campus and overseeing the curriculum design and faculty recruitment. At NYU she previously served as director and Paulette Goddard Professor at the Institute of Fine Arts. She was the associate director of research at the Clark Art Institute and first received tenure at Rutgers University. A historian of Netherlandish art, Westermann is the author of *A Worldly Art: The Dutch Republic 1585–1718* (1996), *The Amusements of Jan Steen: Comic Painting in the Seventeenth Century* (1997), *Rembrandt—Art and Ideas* (2000), and numerous articles. She has edited five books, including *Anthropologies of Art* (2005). Her museum work includes her *Rijksmuseum Dossier: Johannes Vermeer* (2004) and *Art and Home: Dutch Interiors in the Age of Rembrandt* (Denver Art Museum and Newark Museum, 2001). She is preparing an exhibition on Gardens of Eden. Westermann earned a B.A. at Williams College and a Ph.D. at NYU's Institute of Fine Arts. She has received support from the American Philosophical Society, Center for Advanced Study in the Visual Arts, Clark Art Institute, and National Endowment for the Humanities. She is a trustee of MASS MoCA, the Little Red School House, the International Alliance for the Protection of Heritage in Conflict Zones (ALIPH), and the Institute of International Education and its Scholar Rescue Fund.

INDEX

Aaron, 119
Achebe, Chinua. 65, 71; *No Longer at Ease*, 65, 71
acupuncture, 136
Adelson, Sheldon, 52
admiration, 136
Aeschylus, 88
aesthetics, 91, 96, 134, 136–37, 142
Agamben, Giorgio, 121, 129–30
Agyeman-Duah, Ivor, 43; *Bu Me Be: Proverbs of the Akan*, 42–43
al-Asaad, Khaled, 120
Albinoni, Tomaso, 89
allegory, 136
Allen, Danielle, 91
Almahfoud, Bashar, 125
American Academy of Arts and Sciences, 21–22, 55, 82, 108, 128, 133
American Dialect Society, 87
American Historical Association, 85
amphibian, 136
Anderson, Tanisha, 59
Andrew W. Mellon Foundation, 108, 112, 128, 142
anti-intellectualism, 15, 94–95, 104–5; Anti-Smarts, 5, 93–94
Appiah, K. Anthony, 4, 12, 21–22, 25, 43, 90, 139; *Bu Me Be: Proverbs of the Akan*, 43
Appiah, Peggy, 43, 139; *Bu Me Be: Proverbs of the Akan*, 43
Arab Spring, 17
Arac, Jonathan, 78
Archias, 4, 28–29, 41, 43
Arendt, Hannah, 61, 71, 114–15, 117–18, 121, 127, 129–30; *The Origins of Totalitarianism*, 115, 130
Aristophanes, 75; *The Clouds*, 75
Aristotle, 26, 136
art, 4–6, 7, 11–12, 18, 25–27, 30–31, 34–35, 41–43, 46, 89–90, 93–94, 96, 98–99, 108, 114, 117, 119, 122–23, 125–27, 133, 135–38
artists, 135–36, 142

Aubrey, John, 37
Austen, Jane, 32

Baldwin, James, 71–72, 88; "A Talk to Teachers," 88
Bachmann, Michele, 93
Barthes, Roland, 135–37
Bashō, Matsuo, 27–28
beauty, 5, 73, 76, 86, 89, 136
Beck, Glenn, 94
Becker, Carl, 85, 91
Belkin, Douglas, 55
Benjamin, Walter, 136
Betts, Alexander, 129–30
Big Data, 9, 49
Black Lives Matter movement, 88; #All Lives Matter, 58, 67; #BlackLivesMatter, 58, 87–88, 91
Bland, Sandra, 59
Boycott, Divestment, and Sanctions movement, 60
Boyer, Ernest L., 19–20, 22
Boyd, Rekia, 59
Braidotti, Rosi, 20, 22
Brexit, 9–10
Boal, Augusto, 136–38
Bobo, Lawrence D., 59, 62, 71–72
Bourdieu, Pierre, 29, 43
Boyer, Ernest L., 19, 20, 22
Brown Jr., Michael, 4, 59, 87
Buddha (Siddhartha Gautama), 27
Burke, Kenneth, 77, 90–91
Bush, George W., 96

Calexit, 9, 21, 23
Calleson, Diane C., 19, 22
Calvino, Italo, 137
Campion, Edmund, 33
Cantor, Nancy, 19, 22
Carpaccio, Vittore, 37
Carr, Nicholas, 6, 94, 104
Cartonera, 137
Castillo, David, 93, 104, 139
catharsis, 136